The Use of Force

John Brown Ed.D.

The Use of Force

Teaching Adolescents in the 21st Century

PETER LANG
New York - Berlin - Bruxelles - Chennai - Lausanne - Oxford

Library of Congress Cataloging-in-Publication Data

Names: Brown, John, author.
Title: The use of force: teaching adolescents in the 21st century / John Brown.
Other titles: Teaching adolescents in the twenty-first century
Description: New York: Peter Lang, [2024] | Includes bibliographical references and index.
Identifiers: LCCN 2024010268 (print) | LCCN 2024010269 (ebook) |
ISBN 9781636675305 (paperback; alk. paper) | ISBN 9781636675312 (pdf) | ISBN 9781636675329 (epub)
Subjects: LCSH: Education, Secondary—Evaluation. | Affective education. | Mindfulness (Psychology) | Student growth (Academic achievement) | Teacher-student relationships. | Teachers—Training of.
Classification: LCC LB2822.75. B784 2024 (print) | LCC LB2822.75 (ebook) | DDC 373—dc23/eng/20240422
LC record available at https://lccn.loc.gov/2024010268
LC ebook record available at https://lccn.loc.gov/2024010269
DOI 10.3726/b21781

Bibliographic information published by the Deutsche Nationalbibliothek.
The German National Library lists this publication in the German
National Bibliography; detailed bibliographic data is available
on the Internet at http://dnb.d-nb.de.

Cover design by Peter Lang Group AG

ISBN 9781636675305 (paperback)
ISBN 9781636675312 (ebook)
ISBN 9781636675329 (epub)
DOI 10.3726/b21781

© 2024 Peter Lang Group AG, Lausanne
Published by Peter Lang Publishing Inc., New York, USA
info@peterlang.com - www.peterlang.com

All rights reserved.
All parts of this publication are protected by copyright.
Any utilization outside the strict limits of the copyright law, without the permission of the publisher, is forbidden and liable to prosecution.
This applies in particular to reproductions, translations, microfilming, and storage and processing in electronic retrieval systems.

This publication has been peer reviewed.

My father shared this dream with me.
This book is dedicated to him.
John A. Brown (1935–2022)

ACKNOWLEDGMENTS

About 10 years ago, I held an informal meeting of teachers made up of former students, colleagues, and former colleagues—all teachers—in my home so we could share our ideas about teaching. At one point in the evening, a former student turned middle school English Language Arts (ELA) teacher asked me when I would put all of my ideas about teaching in one place where she could access them. I shrugged off the suggestion then, but clearly, the idea never left me. And every time a student, former student, or consulting client would ask me if I had ever written a book about my ideas as they relate to teaching, I would say, "Someday maybe."

Well, that day has finally come, and I need to thank a few people for helping me with it, starting with Kelsey Little, who, standing in the corner of my living room that night, was the first person to suggest that I write this book. I also have to thank Bob Cunningham, who used to be my boss and is now an occasional guest speaker in my classes, a fellow scholar of teaching, book editor, fishing buddy, and friend, for not only writing the forward to this book, reviewing it carefully, and helping me along the way, but also for being the very first person to teach me about the consequences of using force in my teaching. Thank you, Bob.

This book would not exist if it were not for some other friends as well.

Thank you, Kayla Nutter, who served as this book's first editor. Your organizational skills made this a better book.

Thank you, Paul Scoglio, who not only helped me "see the book" in my mind but encouraged me every step of the way.

Thank you, Danielle Ricci, for taking the time, energy, and care to read this book carefully during the process.

Thank you, Jay Simmons, for being my boss, sponsor, and role model for my teaching and writing.

Thank you to Joe Salvatore and Debra Anderson, my oldest and closest "writer/teacher friends," for *going there* first and pulling me through.

Thank you to John Donlon, Steve Lentini, Jack O'Keefe, Michael Goddu, and Warren Gibbons for holding me accountable.

Thank you, Jack Schneider, Patrick Larkin, Scarlett Tannetta, Melissa Tse, Jenny Lee, Karina Hanson, and all my former students and colleagues from UMass Lowell, Shawheen Technical High School, and Landmark School. You are the reason for this book.

Thank you, Alison (Ali) Jefferson, my editor at Peter Lang, for understanding my vision for this book and for guiding me through the process.

Thank you to my mother, Judy, and to my father, John, for being my first teachers and for always encouraging me to write down my ideas. To my two sons, Kevin and Connor, who are my newest and now my most powerful teachers. You inspire me every day.

And most importantly to my partner, teacher, best friend, and the most outstanding teacher, Kathleen Murphy, who always gives me the confidence and support to live my life with meaning and purpose and who encourages me to take risks, do hard things, and finish what I have started.

TABLE OF CONTENTS

	Acknowledgments	vii
	Foreword	xi
Chapter 1	The Confessions of a Bad Teacher	1
Chapter 2	Social and Emotional Learning	13
Chapter 3	The Hammer	25
Chapter 4	Intrinsic Motivation	35
Chapter 5	The Compliance-based Model	43
Chapter 6	What Is Pedagogy?	51
Chapter 7	The Gravity of Being	63
Chapter 8	Mindfulness	73

Chapter 9	Force and Trauma	83
Chapter 10	The Problem with "Academic Rigor"	91
Chapter 11	Responding to Force and Fear	99
Chapter 12	Power of Belief	107
Chapter 13	Another Way	117
Chapter 14	The Teachable Moment	131
Chapter 15	The Role of a Teacher	139
	References	149
	Index	157

FOREWORD

When John was teaching at my school, he had to learn how to do it his way because he failed to do it by the numbers. He was not a practitioner who could do that. And his department chair, who was a standards-based educator, was confused by John's approach.

We used to pre- and post-test students using norm-referenced vocabulary and comprehension tests annually, and John's students always tested above his peers in the English Department, above his department chair, too. And he had some of the most academically challenged students in the school.

The department chair would browbeat John, asking, "How is this happening?"

He was confused because John wasn't teaching to the test. John wasn't even using a standards-based approach to his teaching, but his students were growing faster and further than the other teachers in the department, as measured by this objective performance criteria.

John's students' high levels of growth were based on the authenticity of John's practice. Their cognitive, intellectual, and academic development was rooted in an understanding that John shared with them, and they shared with John.

You might say that his students "bought in," but John had to *buy in* as much as they did. They worked, and they worked hard, because they were committed to the activity in that classroom with that instructor. They worked hard because he did. It was not easy for him. John went through hell to get there.

The most powerful element in the successful practice of any teacher is authenticity, and that means that teachers must know themselves and know themselves well, committing to purposes with which they can align themselves. That's what John did. This book reflects the unique mindset he developed and refined over the 16 years he worked for me.

Dr. Robert Cunningham, Former Principal and Assistant Superintendent

· 1 ·

THE CONFESSIONS OF A BAD TEACHER

Some days I wonder how I ever became a teacher. Why? Because it scares me. Teaching is a job that has so much fear embedded in it. Around every corner, there is something that we can be terrified of. I have experienced so many fears over the course of my 25 years as a professional educator that I should have died of a heart attack by now. In a way, I have died—many times. I have died of fear of embarrassment, of failure, of loneliness, of pain, and of shame, as well as of losing my identity. I have died too many times to count, and sometimes I have felt all these fears at the same time.

As truly frightening as teaching was for me in the beginning, even more terrifying were those years when I was a student. With no control over my own schedule and no power to make decisions about what I did, where I did it, how I did it, and who I did it with, my time as a student in K-12 schools was an exercise first in my need for autonomy, which, after being stifled, then became my need to rebel, which, after being suppressed and excoriated, was ultimately eclipsed by my need for survival. The silent and obedient survival skills I achieved in childhood were neither stimulating nor nurturing. I held on to them longer than I needed to. Way too long.

As liberated and freewheeling as the ethos of schools had become when I was in elementary school in the 1970s, compared to the traditional institution of school before and after, teaching was still, at its core, about compliance. This compliance-based schooling originated in a religiosity of thought about behavior that demonized, infantilized, and demeaned children as incomplete, ignorant, and unworthy of having any freedom to choose how, what, and when we learned. This pathological need for control has only gotten worse over time. Teaching is still about compliance.

The longstanding and unshakable tradition of school being about "training" continued through the 1970s, informed by the persistently crude mindset that children are wild and require taming, one that the founder of educational psychology, Edward Thorndike, used as a rationale to apply behaviorist ideas to teaching. This widely influenced the tradition of schooling in the 20th century and, sadly, still does so today.

As a little kid, learning for me was naturally stimulating, intrinsically motivating, and ultimately satisfying by itself, but in school, it became just something I had to learn to tolerate. I had to swallow lessons whole, accept the realities "taught" without question, and adopt them so I could join various institutions in American society like the economy, upper middle-class culture, and family. Like most people, I was a means for these institutions, a small redundant gear in a giant machine. Being under the thumb of adults and of socially powerful peers ultimately represented a system of control antithetical to my education in every way. What should have been like play for me wasn't; it was just work. It was forceful and even abusive.

Obviously, I survived. Just barely. Ironically, my survival did not free me of the institution, because when I started teaching, at age 22, I lived in constant fear. Thank God, I didn't know how scared I was back then. If I had known, I would never have made it this far, never learned how to be good at it, and never become a real teacher. That would have been very sad, because I love teaching and am good at it. But I didn't always. I have been and sometimes still am afraid of losing the respect of my students, the respect of my colleagues, and the respect of my bosses. When I was a schoolteacher, I was afraid of losing the respect of my students' parents and/or guardians. By "schoolteacher," I mean a K-12 teacher as opposed to a college professor or some other kind of educator. I still occasionally fear losing faith or heart, forgetting a student's name, or making a mistake that will cause a student grief or confusion. I very rarely fear misjudging a teaching situation, damaging my reputation, or getting fired. Those fears have shrunk and are now very small, but fear is clingy and hard to shed. It doesn't matter what we know because fear sticks to us. It is invisible—just barely perceptible—but always there. This is what makes fear so dangerous and alluring as a means of achieving institutional ends.

Discussing our fears is important because it is our fears that define us. They control our lives through the many subconscious behaviors we live out daily. Most of our fears are born in our childhoods, and though this is not always a reality that is obvious to us, it is true, and it is a truth that if we ignore it, we do so at our own peril. The best teachers figure out what they are afraid of and why, because we learn that it is our fears that block access to our creativity, identity, compassion, and building relationships with our students. We must trace our fears back to the traumas in our lives. Those events and experiences that in our childhoods wounded us deeply define us. And if we don't relive them, examine them, and reflect on their power, one day we will simply find ourselves unable to teach.

As author and psychologist Mark Epstein writes in *The Trauma of Everyday Life*, "Trauma does not just happen to a few unlucky people; it is the bedrock of our psychology. Death and illness touch us all, but even the everyday sufferings of loneliness and fear are traumatic."

When that day comes, and it does for most teachers, most of us do not quit our jobs, but we do stop teaching, and we stop learning. That means we may never feel the joy that comes from those moments when we connect with our students, inspire them to dream, and help them accomplish those dreams. As convenient as it would be for me to say that "on that day" teachers choose to be teachers or burnouts, who merely pretend to teach, the phenomena are far more complex. When that day comes, we don't simply quit. The effect is more subtle; instead, we break our own rules and chip our souls into tiny little pieces, selling the pieces off one day at a time just to get by. It is a slow death, like a thousand tiny cuts. We become less curious at first, then less spontaneous. We replace wonder with strategy. We become calculating, risk-averse, and political. We listen to our creative and spirited inner voice less and less and turn to voices of conventional wisdom, adopting deficit thinking. We develop a scarcity mindset and play life as a *zero-sum game*. Surrounded by voices repeating conventional wisdom, telling us cautionary tales that cool our passions, stifle our innovation, and extinguish curiosity, sympathy, and imagination, we are socialized into becoming parts of a whole, slowly cashing out whatever currently make us individuals to pay for sins for which we are innocent.

It happens little by little, hour by hour. This is how a teacher's soul dies. It happens all the time. First, we discover how to survive a day of teaching, then we achieve success, measured by external—someone else's—standards. After that, we attempt to protect the success that we have won as if it were a precious thing that could be lost, taken, or mistaken. Ironically, it is our very attempts to protect our prized success that prevent real success from ever manifesting. Without our souls, we lose trust in our intuition and make planning, control, and methodology more important than care, attention, and patience. The implementation of our most conservative and strategic plans becomes more important than our students.

I was bullied when I was a child in elementary school. I eventually buried those experiences and the feelings that went with them and tried to paint over them to erase them, but trauma cannot be completely erased, and healing does not occur by ignoring disease. Our subconscious minds record everything that happens to us, and our bodies remember those experiences, even when our conscious minds do not. When I became a teacher at 22 years old, I had no idea that those bullies would come back to haunt me in adulthood. They did. They came back to haunt me at the moments when I was at my weakest, when I most needed to be strong. In those moments, every one of them was in the classroom. They came back while I was with my students. I felt as if they could see those bullies standing right there in the room.

Bullies, as children or adults, instinctively rely on fear to enhance the level of force they can exercise. And this blend of fear and force, whether linguistic or physical, is violent, especially for a child. The trauma that lives on in that person inhibits their growth and makes them susceptible to becoming violent themselves. At the same time, the bullies become addicted to the power they feel when they know they can force other people to do what they want. Though bullies are not the most sympathetic characters in our stories, they are victims too. We all are.

Those bullies became internalized in me; even though the threat they represented to me as a child was gone, they lived inside me, feeding on a fear that was always there—even before they went to work on me—and force seemed like the only way to fight them. It was all I knew. I tried to push their voices and their meanness out of my mind and out of my dreams. I tried to be the opposite, gentle and kind, but I fell into an unconscious state whenever I witnessed that meanness in my students or in other kids, in the hallways or at lunch. Even when I did manage to be conscious of this dynamic and stifle my impulses to overreact, I would use all the mental force of will that I could muster to bully myself, controlling my impulses to bully the bullies.

Questions about my ability to teach and doubts about my worth as a person crept into my consciousness early on, as if the ghosts of my childhood bullies could see an opening in a moment of weakness where I was using force against myself. This would happen in my classroom during many lessons. I could not teach when this happened. I also could not effectively deal with the bullying I was witnessing. Unable to compassionately teach those bullies who were right in front of me to not give into their baser instincts, I would either become paralyzed or overreact. Consequently, I was also unable to protect the victims of the bullying and help them heal, all of which I discovered years later was *teaching*. They call it social and emotional learning (SEL) now. The bottom line here is that I failed to teach my students some of the most important lessons because this toxic mix of hyper-protection and hyper-transference caused pain, distracting me from my mission, making me selfish, and falsely causing me to believe that I had to choose between being forced or being forceful, between being afraid and being feared.

Emotionally triggered, I was raw, naked, vulnerable, and weak. With confidence gone and self-efficacy drained away, I was not able to be an effective role model of strength and resilience. I was neither self-aware nor self-possessed, both of which are necessary for teaching SEL. Immediately after such a triggering event, and for the rest of that day, I would be useless to myself and to my students. I would hide somewhere inside myself where the old bullies, ghosts from my own past, and the new bullies, my students, could not find me, and where the bully in me could not find me either. I was lost. I was unavailable for my students.

As much as I hate to admit it, and I never planned to do it, I did sometimes bully the bullies in my classroom, in the hallways, and at lunch, which means I bullied my own students. I lied to myself and said that I was preventing more bullying by punishing those bullies and getting justice for those they bullied. But that was not what I was really doing. I was trying to protect a wounded part of me that had retreated so deeply inside. My unconscious fear led to my becoming forceful. Sometimes I ask myself, "Was it just misplaced revenge for what the bullies did to me when I was a child, so many years ago?"

I suppose so. But then, what is revenge but a screwed-up rebalancing of power originating from transference that we were only vaguely aware of at the time? I became forceful, thinking it was the only way to wrestle my power back. Every time I witnessed the same brand of meanness in the school where I worked that had crushed me when I was a helpless little boy, I could not help but identify with those victims. No longer a little boy, I used my enormous personal, social, cognitive, and political powers and my position of adult authority to do more than defend the victims, more than protect the vulnerable, and more than teach the bullies, whose acts of meanness probably were born of their own scarred-over wounds. I could hurt them. And I am sure I did. I did not know I had all that power, because I still felt more weak than strong. I realize now that I possessed enormous power, and I used and even abused it.

It wasn't until I faced these facts, remembered the events of my childhood, and finally felt those feelings from way back then, when I was bullied through most of elementary school and middle school, that I could begin to heal and then help my students who were the victims of bullying, to prevent bullying events, and even teach the bullies how not to be so cruel. Most of them were the victims of someone's excessive use of force, like I was. Like me, they might learn to resist the urge to become perpetrators. They too might learn to reflect on their experiences and their feelings, understand the effects that their forceful behaviors have on others and on themselves, and know what force does to us instead of wielding it unconsciously. Fear of the self, of weakness, of being seen as a victim, and of being victimized once again prevented me from being a good teacher to my students, some of whom were bullies, like I had become, and some of whom were victims, like I had been. Somewhere, we learn that the best way to protect ourselves from bullies is to become more powerful than them. Power corrupts and as Nietzsche said so eloquently, "He who fights with monsters might take care lest he thereby become a monster. And if you gaze for long into an abyss, the abyss gazes also into you."

Even today, I still have the capacity to be a monster, and when I remember this fact, I think of this quotation from Hiam Ginott:

> I've come to a frightening conclusion that I am the decisive element in the classroom. It's my personal approach that creates the climate. It's my daily mood that makes the weather. As a teacher, I possess a tremendous power to make a child's life miserable or joyous. I can be a tool of torture or an instrument of inspiration. I can humiliate or heal. In all situations, it is my response that decides whether a crisis will be escalated or de-escalated, and a child humanized or dehumanized.
>
> *Between parent and child*, 1965

In my early years as a teacher, I would spend all day Sunday dreading Monday because I was afraid of my students. Or was I afraid of failure? Maybe I was afraid of being wrong? Of course, I was afraid of both being wrong and of failing. I was also afraid I would make a mistake in front of my students, which came from a fear of not being perfect. I was afraid of being caught not knowing my subject area. I taught English. They call it *ELA* these days. And there is quite a lot to not know about *ELA*. I could not know a grammar rule, the correct spelling of a word, or the meaning of a word. I might mispronounce a word or not be familiar with a particular work of literature. I could be confused about the meaning of a poem or a story. I could be ignorant of the history of some aspects of the English language. The list goes on. And on. Every subject area has far too much of its own "content literacy" to ever completely master, and we are all in danger of being overwhelmed with insecurity. I was arrogant, too. And egocentric. I was so self-absorbed that I had not considered that other teachers, even good teachers, don't know everything that they might be afraid to admit it to even themselves.

I was also afraid of being speechless, which my students would laugh at now because they can't shut me up. At one time, I was also scared that I might be put in a position where I would be forced to respond to something and not know what to say. I was afraid I would be found out for the fraud I was. I would be caught making a mistake, not knowing, and punished for it. I was terrified that I would be alone, abandoned, and left unsupported in my classroom all by myself. I was afraid of shame, pain, criticism, and disappointing other people who counted on me. I was afraid that I could be physically hurt by one of my students or by a stranger.

I was afraid that I cared too much about my students and not enough about the *ELA* curriculum. I cared too much about what my bosses thought of me, which made me scared they would catch me "not teaching." And I was afraid that my colleagues would not respect me. I was also afraid that I was not meeting my students' needs, maybe because, I was afraid my own needs would not be met or because as a child, they sometimes weren't. I was terrified that my students thought I was boring, stupid, or foolish. I feared that they would not listen, almost as much as I feared they would never talk. I feared that my students would perform poorly on standardized tests.

I was afraid of the other, the unpredictable and of losing control of the classroom, which I realized later was an unsolvable problem because facing that which is alien is just as much a part of the job as accepting the unpredictable nature of reality and the fact that control is an illusion. Now, I not only accept the unexpected in my teaching, but I embrace it. I long for the adventure now, am excited by the challenge, and thrive in the most chaotic circumstances.

I still fear intimacy as much as disconnection, boredom as much as overstimulation, and being seen as much as being invisible. I still fear losing my voice as a teacher—not literally, but rather my ability to speak my truth. At times, I have lost my voice. Sometimes I still do. Yet, I am just as scared that I have said too much and been too bold, revealing more than people want to know or can deal with.

I have managed to stop caring about what my bosses think about me or my teaching once I realized that they really don't know what they are doing any more than I do, even if they pretend to, or even if they think they do. I stopped caring about my students' standardized test scores, mostly because my students performed well on them compared to their peers, despite my utter and stubbornly intentional lack of test prep, but also because I understood that teachers have little control over their students' performance on everything from standardized tests to whether they decide to bring their books to class. And I learned that our lack of control extends to many aspects of our work. Once I learned that my control over students is not merely an illusion but an institutionalized myth and that our attempts to control are wrongheaded, rolled up in the system's expectations of us, I stopped worrying about my failure and my students' failure. I began to understand that failure was not only inevitable but also necessary.

My fear of being wrong finally relaxed when a new belief developed in me that dualism is not practical. And it certainly is not a thought process I want to model for my students. I was less afraid of making mistakes in front of my students. Instead, I used my mistakes to model for them how to learn from failure. My fear of not being perfect eventually dissolved into an acceptance that everything was going to be okay, and that was enough. I was no longer afraid of being thought of as a teacher who doesn't know ELA. That fear was replaced by a radical honesty: I am not "the" teacher who doesn't know ELA. I am "a" teacher who doesn't know ELA, and instead of that fact triggering feelings of insecurity, I was inspired to enter a growing (now continuous) state of curiosity about what I don't know and how to acquire that knowledge.

It's liberating to let go of the unrealistic expectations we sometimes put on ourselves that we must be all-knowing experts about our subject areas. Giving that up earned me more respect from my students, not less. It also allowed me to build relationships more easily with them, which made me a better teacher in the long run. When my colleagues realized I didn't know this or that about ELA and were surprised and sometimes judgmental, I shrugged, knowing that I was doing the best I could and that they weren't perfect either.

I learned that suddenly realizing I did not remember a specific grammar rule while teaching a lesson on writing was an opportunity for me and my students to investigate that grammar rule together instead of feeling shame and trying to hide. I still make spelling errors, and I have learned to laugh at this with my students, which only helps them feel less uptight about their own imperfections. When I learned about a work of literature that I had not read, I very publicly would say "I have never read that," and then I would write that title and author on our booklist, which was a whiteboard that hung on the wall of our classroom with the titles of many books, poems, and plays I hadn't yet read. I learned to embrace my confusion and my ignorance about the meaning of a poem or a story, thus using such a moment to be vulnerable with my students. After all, I remembered being a high school student who had teachers who seemed to be so well read, intelligent, and educated that I was intimidated by the sheer depth of their knowledge instead of curious and inspired by it.

I am somewhat ignorant of the history of the English language. So what? I am not a master of my content area, nor do I want to be. I am not an expert writer, reader, or literary critic. At one point, I adopted the phrase "nobody's perfect" as my mantra. I would say it aloud in front of my students, and it was liberating as all hell for both me and for my students. My egocentrism melted into a curiosity about my students' lives, interests, struggles, and goals, but that only happened after I let go of all those expectations that I heaped on myself, that other people were putting on me, or that I assumed they were putting on me. My fear of not meeting those expectations blocked my ability to see my students, to be with them, and to enjoy teaching them. Fear is utterly egocentric. When we are scared, we won't "make it" through the day or even a class period without being found out as a fraud, an imposter, or the dude they hired by mistake. We are defensive, pretentious, closed-minded, and self-absorbed. We get stuck in survival mode, never getting out of our way to see the imperfectly beautiful world we live in. We lie, cover up our mistakes, and highlight our accomplishments, and we become addicted to the affirmation of others.

Fear blocks our access to our own hearts and minds, and if we can't access our emotions and intellects, there is no way our students will let us into theirs. When I was afraid someone—a student, parent, colleague, or my department chair—would catch me making a mistake, I was worried about me. Me, me, me. And the crazy part was that I so deeply feared being punished for not knowing what to do, not knowing the curriculum, or not knowing how to teach that I became bad at responding to situations, anxious about exploring the curriculum, and rigid about my teaching methods, basing them mostly on what I thought my bosses wanted and what I thought was working. I became risk-averse while expecting my students to take academic risks. I was a hypocrite.

Eventually, I discovered that teachers are rarely punished for not knowing what or how to teach. Many years later, I became president of the teacher's union at my school and learned that even the rare incompetent, ignorant, and even lazy teachers don't get fired, at least not right away. I was none of those things. When incompetent, ignorant, or lazy teachers were held accountable, the consequences amounted to some boss explaining to them that they needed to clean up their act. That was all. It was then that I realized I had wasted so much time being anxious about my boss thinking I was a bad teacher, which prevented me from being creative, passionate, and authentic, which are the qualities of the best teachers. These are the toughest qualities to develop.

It's a shame that I wasted so much time fearing teaching, but it makes sense that I fell into that trap because of all the "effective methods" we are taught in teacher school, all the "best practices" that we learn in professional development (PD) workshops, and all the "great lessons" our mentors modeled for us. Among them, *fear* is *the* most commonly used technique in teaching. The compliance-based model of teaching, which is hidden in plain sight, relies on fear to force students to do what we want them to do, to do what our bosses want them to do, and to do what policymakers want them to do.

Ultimately, though, if I had not been such a shitty teacher, I never would have become a real teacher. Many teachers in schools today and many who have taught over the millennia have been run-of-the-mill, crappy teachers. They stick to what they know, daring not to question a system that reinforces their authority as "teachers," because that authority is alluring and intoxicating, masking our infinite ignorance and insecurity. I was not any old "run of the mill" shitty teacher though. When I do crappy, I do it big. I was so bad at teaching, blinded by even the smallest illusion of power, but I was also a failure at adopting the lie that teachers are better than students. I became compelled to take a long, hard look at my behavior, my relationships, and my beliefs, and what I saw was more than just my own character flaws, though there were plenty of those. I saw that the compliance-based teaching that was at the heart of the systems that taught me and that I had bought into as a teacher made me not only ineffective as a teacher but a bad teacher.

Once I got a peek at the below-deck workings of the accepted tradition of using force and fear to further "educational" ends that are external to students, I could not unsee their omnipotence. More than a frequency illusion, these workings became a menacing synchronicity, a poisoned pit, radiating a reality that made me anxious and ill-at-ease. I realized that I could not unsee inhibition, the emotional damage, the abuse of power, and the personal pain that stem from using force and fear in teaching. I knew I would have to go below deck and dismantle it in me. I had to dig up the roots of this weed where it was embedded in my beliefs about learning. I chose to replace force and fear with love, trust, freedom, care, curiosity, intuition, spontaneity, vulnerability, passion, authenticity, creativity, honesty, and acceptance, most of which I had little experience with.

· 2 ·

SOCIAL AND EMOTIONAL LEARNING

"When we care for others, we do not try to motivate them by threats, sanctions, invidious comparisons, and harsh penalties. We do not ignore the expressed needs and varied talents of students and insist on a deadly standardization."

Nel Noddings, *The Challenge to Care in Schools*

What is social and emotional learning?

SEL is the integration of cognitive and affective domains in children so they can gain and apply the knowledge and skills they need to manage their emotions, set socially acceptable goals, and feel and express empathy for other people.

This helps students to develop and manage positive relationships. Some educators will tell you that SEL is a new program their school is using to satisfy the auditors who evaluate their school for accreditation. SEL is about much more than compliance, and it is not new. Good teachers have been teaching SEL for decades, both explicitly and by example. Teaching and learning do not happen without SEL. It involves developing an *ethic of care* in schools and classrooms. The stated goal of SEL programming is to prepare students to become responsible, caring members of society, and that makes sense, but those goals aside (who doesn't believe in developing responsible and caring people?) SEL is inseparable from academic instruction and cognitive development, which is why teachers have been using SEL as a means just as much as an end for over 50 years.

Why does SEL matter?

SEL helps adolescents recognize and understand their own feelings, which is a necessary precondition for the appropriate expression of those emotions, for having empathy toward others, and for building relationships. Adolescents' mental health, social skills, and academic achievement all depend on SEL. The benefits students experience from SEL last for months and even years. Academic outcomes and student well-being are increased, and negative outcomes like emotional distress, drug abuse, and sexually transmitted diseases among adolescents are decreased with SEL. Research conducted by Mark Greenberg at *The Learning Policy Institute* in 2023 shows that with conscious SEL implementation:

- student achievement is improved
- student mental, physical, and emotional health and wellness are improved
- classroom behavior is improved
- problem behaviors are reduced
- academic outcomes are improved
- students manage stress better
- student depression and anxiety are reduced
- self-efficacy is improved
- students learn decision-making skills
- students build relationship skills
- conflicts are reduced among students
- students become more self-aware
- students learn self-management strategies
- students become more socially aware and sympathetic
- students develop better self-regulation

What is the best way to include SEL in our classrooms?

The most powerful way that we can integrate SEL into our classrooms is to see our classes as communities and our students as people. When we build supportive and safe learning environments in our classrooms, we make it possible for our students to grow as people. Nobody grows cognitively without growing emotionally, socially, and psychologically. These aspects are not distinct from each other. They are twisted together in the most profound and complex patterns and designs. Building community requires leadership in its purest form.

If we create a sense of belonging for all our students, we will satisfy their needs for social acceptance and validation, both of which are prerequisites for sustainable education. This requires us to set explicit boundaries for student behavior so that students will be able to predict that their participation will be honored, not belittled. All students must feel emotionally safe before they can learn. When I was a high school English teacher, my approach to setting boundaries became more collaborative with each passing year. I worked with my students to develop our class expectations. They created expectations for me, for themselves, and for each other.

I would begin this process at the beginning of each school year with each class—not the first day, but during the first week. I would ask my students, most of whom were new to me, and I would ask them what they should expect of me. Often, I would use an ungraded quick write at the start of class to get us started. Five minutes later, I would ask for volunteers to read what they wrote, and I would listen carefully, sometimes writing with their permission their responses on the board or on the data projector. Other times, I would have them write them on post-it notes and stick them on the board. I would never compel students to read their responses. To force them is a violation of everything that SEL stands for.

More often than not, they would write that they expect me to be fair and responsible, not to play favorites, not to be mean, and to be sensitive and reasonable. They wouldn't say so directly, but they wanted me to trust them.

Trusting teenagers who I didn't even know did not come easy to me at first, but after a few years, I realized I had more to lose by not trusting all of them than by placing my trust in them and having one or two students take advantage of that trust. I did not loan any of them my car or give them the password to my email, but I found that it was easier for me to trust them than for them to trust me. So, I had to go first. And the more I trusted them, the more they trusted me. I also found that when we had some level of trust, which, of course, was different for each student, I had to protect that trust as sacred, and they, in turn, tried not to violate the trust I placed in them. Sometimes, when students thought that they may have lost my trust, they would be visibly disappointed in themselves. That's how much they valued our trust, but it started with me. Trust is about safety, and students can't learn without feeling safe.

Working together with students on the norms (expectations) we would live by that school year provided us the opportunity to practice cooperation and for me to prove my egalitarianism. We would together build the learning community they needed. The more honest I was, the more honest they were. The more patient I was, the more patient my students were. Teachers are powerful models. Our students may not immediately display the behaviors that they learn from our example, but we nearly always find that they do so eventually. And, when they do not, if we reflect on our own behavior, we will often find that we have sent them a mixed message somewhere along the way. We are not perfect. We do our best. As I often tell the college students I teach now who want to be teachers, whatever your students see you do, they will do too. So be aware of what you model.

Despite adult culture's attempt to demonize them, adolescents are not bad people, not lazy, and not stupid either. They are doing the best they can during the most volatile years of their lives. And just like us, they are not perfect. So, together, we would make our class expectations into a guiding document, and I found that if we met monthly, sometimes weekly as needed, to check on the status of our evolving *relationship as a community*, we could change, adjust, and reinforce that document to reflect the needs of *our community* if we needed to.

Maslow

Most of the ideas that I grounded my ethic of care in over my years teaching came from the ideas of educational psychologist, Abraham Maslow. Maslow, a professor at Columbia University, Brooklyn College, and The New School for Social Research in New York City, is known for his theories of motivation and performance, and for popularizing the concept of *self-actualization*. In 1951, after studying under noted German psychologist, Alfred Adler, at Columbia, Maslow explained *self-actualization* as a person's overwhelming desire for fulfillment, identifying their human potential and then achieving it. This can be thought of as a desire to become everything that we are capable of being. Maslow's idea is that once a person reaches this level, he or she becomes self-motivated and self-disciplined and adopts a more internal locus of control. When we think of a person who is driven, who enjoys the hard work that goes into making themselves successful, and who masters specific skills, that is self-actualization. Think Tom Brady, Serena Williams, Misty Copeland, Barack Obama, Sting, Robin Williams, and Oprah Winfrey. By extension, Maslow's work led him to develop a schema that explained how the satisfaction of different kinds of needs at different levels gives us access to higher and higher levels of growth. He organized this theory into what he called the *hierarchy of needs.* An individual who reaches the highest levels of satisfaction with their needs can attain what he termed an "optimal state."

Maslow's research helped him conclude that self-actualized people have the following traits in common:

- see reality as it is
- accept their flaws and the flaws of others
- are independent and spontaneous
- are resourceful
- feel gratitude for simple things in life
- have deep, loving bonds with others
- value solitude
- laugh at themselves
- are compassionate
- are interested in community and humanity
- are not easily shamed
- have a few close friends rather than many acquaintances
- sometimes feel at one with the universe

Maslow's Hierarchy of Needs

Though Maslow never envisioned a pyramid, he did not argue with it when he saw his theory framed as such. The most fundamental needs are at the bottom of the pyramid, and the need for identity and fulfillment is at the top. His theory holds that people's pursuit of our most basic needs occupy most of our daily lives. Since then, many writers and other thinkers have written that Maslow thought that the basic needs had to be met before we could achieve other needs higher up on the pyramid, like a feeling of belonging or sense of accomplishment. And, although this is an important question, it, like the frame of a pyramid, was someone else's extension of Maslow's theory.

Nevertheless, the four basic layers of the pyramid are what Maslow called the "deficiency needs." They are esteem, belonging and acceptance, safety, and physical needs like air, food, and rest. If the deficiencies are not met, the person feels anxious and tense. Imagine that you have not had breakfast, and then you go to do a CrossFit workout. You won't have the fuel you need to physically do the workout. Or, you got three hours of sleep last night, and then you take a test for your teacher's license. Your mind, deprived of the essential rest it needs, will not be able to perform complex cognitive tasks. Maslow did not directly state that our most basic levels of need must be met before we can even want the higher-level needs. This is an interpretation that other theorists have made of his work. However, it is an interesting question, considering what we know about our students' capacities as teachers. For example, we know that when our students are not completing their assigned work, when they are not following directions or rules, if they are not making an effort to accomplish academic tasks—not fulfilling their potential—we know this does not mean that they are bad people or that we are bad teachers. We know that they are distracted by their unfulfilled needs, and their hunger.

Often, we find that when our students' self-efficacy is low—or their need for rest, safety, or belonging has not been met—they falter. Sometimes our cultural programming urges us to judge these students as lazy, disruptive, and lacking in self-discipline. But, upon reflection, we know that motivation, cooperation, and self-discipline require us to be undistracted by our deficiencies. So, why is it not the same for our students? We may find it easy to judge other people (our students, in particular) for their behaviors because their unmet needs are not visible to us.

Motivation is complex, and various aspects of one's psyche operate on multiple levels of Maslow's hierarchy simultaneously. As teachers, it is very difficult to know what our students need when, which is why trust is so important. If they trust us, they can communicate their needs. But if we are hyper-focused on academic content and skills, testing, and compliance, trust can be lost unintentionally.

A staple of curriculum and teaching academic subjects has for decades been another pyramid, but in the past 15 years, this other pyramid has been rolled out anew by edugurus, curriculum consultants, academics, and school leaders. This other pyramid is called *Bloom's Taxonomy*. The problem is that children cannot access the skills on Bloom's hierarchy until they have their needs met on Maslow's first.

Benjamin Bloom

In 1956, an educational psychologist at the University of Chicago named Benjamin Bloom led the development of a classification system for educational objectives. This was part of his strategy for teaching mastery of various academic subjects. At the heart of this classification system was a scheme that taxonomized different domains in a person, but the one domain that describes types of thinking, the cognitive domain, like remembering, applying skills, and analyzing concepts, has come to eclipse the other two domains. The other two domains are the affective domain and the psychomotor domain. Eventually, the skills in the cognitive domain were shaped into a pyramid like Maslow's. Today, *Bloom's Taxonomy* (minus the affective and psychomotor domains) is ubiquitous in K-12 curriculum work.

The affective domain is related to the individual's emotions. This is the basis for SEL. The psychomotor domain concerns itself with the relationship between cognitive behavior and physical activity. Although the goal of taxonomies is to separate the domains from one another so we can understand human behavior through analytical thought, especially those aspects that affect learning, Bloom (1956) never even implied that they are inherently separate. Quite the opposite. He wrote that they are fully integrated within each of us. We must not take them as distinct from one another in our understanding of our students.

It is precisely the denial of the affective and psychomotor domains in service of academic outcomes, through our hyper-attention to the cognitive domain over the past few decades that has led educators more recently to see the need for SEL and advocate for it, even on a political level. Outcome-obsessed policymakers, politicians, captains of industry, academics, and school administrators have finally begun to accept that without taking care of our students' affective and psychomotor domains, without taking care of our students' most basic needs, academic outcomes plateau, and the consequences of denying their deficiency needs are often destructive.

Bloom's Taxonomy is a hierarchical epistemology that classifies human thinking so that educational objectives can be carefully considered and categorized. The deeper education policy has focused on academic outcomes (i.e., standards-based curriculum, high-stakes testing, and system evaluation based on test scores), the farther away we as teachers have strayed from the other two domains and from Maslow's theory about what brings students' attention to accomplishing those objectives in the first place. A recent and significant increase in mental illness, emotional disorders, addiction, and antisocial behavior among adolescents is likely related to education systems' moving away from students' emotional needs, and SEL activists, like *The Social and Emotional Learning Alliance of the United States* (SEL4US), argue that it is likely a contributing factor. They advocate for a return to teaching SEL, and policies are quickly being developed, legislation is being passed, and investments are being made toward this end, but the injection of new SEL standards is not the teaching of SEL. Time and space need to be made for SEL, but policymakers have not yet allocated this time and this space because they resist any compromise of the high academic standards they set and invested in for school achievement, which they believe are necessary for economic growth. American public schools cannot afford to make time and resources available for anything more than a token nod toward SEL because they are accountable for high levels of performance on high-stakes standardized tests. There is no indication that policymakers will give ground to teaching SEL at the expense of academic standards. So, instead, they heap the SEL standards atop all the other initiatives they push on schools, cheapening every one of them all the while. And so, it is up to teachers to acknowledge and act in the moment when addressing students' deficiencies.

Maslow's Hierarchy of Needs must be considered BEFORE Bloom's Taxonomy

Popular educulture, driven by teachers, has now latched onto a new mantra: "Maslow before Bloom." This mindset represents long-overdue progress in how we think about teaching and learning. After all, we, humans, children especially, do not expend energy on a task unless we know that:

1. Our deficiency needs are met first. Deficiency needs, part of Maslow's theory, are described as our most basic physiological needs (food, air, warmth, sex, and sleep) and safety needs (security from environmental harm and freedom from danger or attack). Deficiency needs are driven by deprivation, where the lack of their basic satisfaction directs us away from other motives and toward our survival. Our need to fulfill these becomes more influential with time. The longer we are deprived, the hungrier we get. In 1943, Maslow explained in an issue of the journal *Psychological Review* his ideas that people cannot progress to meet their higher-level growth needs until they first satisfy lower-level deficit needs. Maslow (1987) later added that he intended the nuance of his theory to be understood and that this sequence of our satisfaction of any deficiency need is not an absolute phenomenon. When our basic survival needs are mostly satisfied, the pressure for us to satisfy them will be reduced, at least temporarily, allowing us to move partially toward meeting growth and other needs. Yet, Maslow believed that

our growth needs are felt just as strongly, if not more strongly, once their satisfaction has been initiated.
2. The task is worth investing our time in. Maslow's 1943 theory of motivation explains that when our needs are not met, the dissatisfaction we feel compels us to move in a new direction, make different decisions, and behave differently in the interest of fulfilling our needs. The new direction and its affiliated behavior are essentially the bedrock of motivation. Since our needs are unconditional, essential, and necessary for our survival, growth, and well-being, we act on these needs first. Hunger, a biological need, requires us to ingest food to maintain life, for example. Without food, air, water, or warmth, the acquisition of academic knowledge is irrelevant.
3. We believe that we have a reasonable chance of being successful at the task. In 1963, noted Stanford psychologist, Albert Bancura, devised a *theory of self-efficacy* based on his concept that the beliefs we possess will increase or decrease our capacity to execute our intentions, plans, or goals, producing specific personal outcomes. Like confidence, self-efficacy is the quality necessary for us to control our own behavior through intrinsic motivation. This cognitive self-evaluative mechanism influences all of our human experiences, including the goals for which we expend energy, the risks we take, and the achievements we work to attain. This theory of belief-oriented behavior is thought to depend on the various domains of functioning at work at the time as well as the circumstances surrounding the occurrence of our behavior.
4. We can expect that the value of our effort to accomplish the task is equal to our need to accomplish the outcome or our interest in achieving it. Harvard psychologist, David McClelland, proposed his *Theory of Needs* decades after Maslow's first writings on the topic to further explain how our needs for achievement, affiliation, and power influence our decisions and behaviors. Developing it in the 1960s, McClelland explained that we all possess these three types of motivation regardless of our age, sex, race, or culture. He called this "the expectancy value theory of motivation." McClelland focused his theory on our needs for achievement, for affiliation, and for power. Our need for achievement drives us toward skill mastery in relation to a standard. This is our simple drive to succeed in life. Our need for affiliation drives us to make and sustain personal relationships with family, friends, acquaintances, colleagues, and rivals. Our need for power drives us to lead and

affect change within both the social and professional organizations to which we belong. McClelland explained that these three needs are non-sequential yet are used in relation to each other.

Children, adolescents, and adults will perform tasks to comply with force, to protect their survival and their interests, despite the reduction in their human freedom; however, compliance is not a sustainable model for teaching and learning because, once the force or threat of it is removed, we re-establish our freedom to pursue our own goals instead of the goals of others.

Some Examples

If a child is hungry, tired, or cold, he or she will not be able to perform even the easiest academic tasks. If he or she is scared (of being physically or emotionally harmed), learning how to read, do math, or organize ideas and thoughts will be nearly impossible. The part of the brain that dominates all of us during a moment when we perceive threat is the amygdala. This is often called the survival brain. It's one of the oldest parts of the brain. The amygdala controls our ability to detect and assess threats, to fight, to run away, to escape, and to hide from danger.

This is not the part of the brain that remembers ideas, conceptualizes theories, and understands nuance. The amygdala doesn't reflect. It reacts. This is why a sense of safety is critical to a child's ability to learn.

If one of your students feels like an outsider, like he or she does not belong in your class, does not feel visible, acknowledged, or important to you and the other students, his or her needs for respect and belonging are not being met, and he or she will not likely be able to comprehend complex text, apply previously learned ideas or skills, problem-solve, analyze data, or hypothesize. Thus, Maslow must come first. Otherwise, planning, teaching, and assessing based on objectives from *Bloom's Taxonomy* will not only be wasted but also will frustrate both you and your students.

How do we put Maslow first?

Start by building community; get to know your students' names, their personalities, and their lives; and foster trust. This may require you to become vulnerable, to admit to your students that you are not perfect, and to care about them and care *for* them—all while maintaining boundaries that keep you and your students safe from yourselves, one another, and the outside world. Greet each student at the door at the beginning of class every day. Ask them about themselves. Listen to what they tell you. Be curious about them, and expect them to be virtuous, brilliant, and hard-working, even when they seem like they may never be any of those things. See your students. And let them be seen.

A Final Thought

Think of the most creative and productive people you know. Do those people have strong self-esteem? Probably. Do they feel a sense of belonging? Most likely. Do they live in fear? I doubt it. If we want our students to reach the summit of Bloom's mountain, we must first climb Mt. Maslow with them. Otherwise, the climb up Bloom's North Face is not only a waste of time and energy but also a Sisyphean task.

· 3 ·

THE HAMMER

"I suppose it is tempting, if the only tool you have is a hammer, to treat everything as if it were a nail."

Abraham H. Maslow, *Toward a Psychology of Being*

Force is the source of most fear we feel as teachers and the most dangerous tool we use on our own students. Whether our bosses try to force us to teach in a particular way or force us to meet specific curriculum standards, force creates fear. Although our bosses may assume that the fear that force brings motivates us to accomplish their goals, that approach to managing teacher behavior is as wrongheaded as when teachers try to scare their students into performing specific tasks in their classes in the name of learning.

Do you think we don't scare our students? Do you think I'm overstating things?

Maybe.

Maybe not.

Let me ask you this: Why do children come to school? Is it because they love school? Maybe some do. Do *all* of your students love coming to school?

Why do they do their homework? Is it so stimulating that they want to do it?

Why do they sit and listen (or pretend to) as we talk? Are we that interesting? Are they that curious about what we have to say?

Some teachers are interesting. Some homework is stimulating. And some children enjoy going to school. If that were not true, there would be no point trying to untangle this knotted mess, but most children, sooner or later, come to school to perform tasks that we require of them and curb their enthusiasm for freedom and their own curiosity and spontaneity out of compliance.

I wonder how necessary that is. How much force do we need to use in our teaching? And what are the liabilities of making kids do things? Our schools rely on our students to fear the consequences that we—their teachers—can deliver for their noncompliance, just as our bosses depend on our fear of what they might do if we don't follow their directions. Teachers in the 21st century use fear more than any other tool in the box, whether we want to admit it or not, which is absurd since we know that the emotion "fear" is an inefficient motivator. We know that it is antithetical to deep learning. Also known under the names anxiety, nervousness, worry, concern, terror, trepidation, and horror, fear has become the traditional teacher's unspoken co-teacher, enabling our use of force. Because without force, how could we possibly teach? After all, children don't always want to learn, and they need to learn, so we have to make them, right?

Why have we made fear our co-pilot?

It's simple, really. We do it because we have been taught that we need to, and we believe that we must make students learn, especially since we were taught to fear our teachers so they could force us to learn when we were kids. Dating back to the 1700s, our persistent beliefs about domesticating humans at a very young age are captured in the sermons of English theologian, John Wesley when he said, "Why did not you break their will from their infancy? At least do it now; better late than never. It should have been done before they were two years old: It may be done at eight or ten, though with far more difficulty. However, do it now; and accept that difficulty as the just reward for your past neglect."

Hey, it worked for us when we were kids, right?

There is a longstanding tradition of believing that learning can only be achieved through *classical conditioning*. This is a popular method of understanding human behavior based on how we respond to different kinds of stimuli. This simplistic adaptation, applying the law of cause and effect to theories of human motivation, is popular because it is easily understood. But various kinds of human behavior, including learning, cognitive development, and intellectual growth, are anything but simple. The experiments that behaviorists like John Watson, B.F. Skinner, and Ivan Pavlov conducted were performed mostly on animals, not on humans. They were able to train animals to change their behavior and perform simple tasks. Their conclusions have shaped the general public's understanding of human behavior throughout the 20th and 21st centuries, leading most people to think in terms of using punishments and rewards to change behavior. Learning is, in fact, a change in behavior. However, it is so complex that there are at least a dozen distinct learning theories.

It seems that we have not yet considered that the lessons we want children to learn are not as simple as those learned by mice navigating a puzzle to find food or dogs that learn to salivate at the sound of a bell. Noted Harvard Psychologist William James explained in his lectures to The Cambridge Schoolteachers in 1899 that "The wise teacher will use this instinct (intellectual sense) as he uses others, reaping its advantages, and appealing to it in such a way as to reap a maximum of benefit with a minimum of harm; for, after all, we must confess… that the deepest spring of action in us is the sight of action in another. The spectacle of effort is what awakens and sustains our own effort."

Unfortunately, because in the most easily and immediately observable ways, the behaviorists' explanations for why we do what we do and how we can change the behavior of other people seem to be valid, and more sophisticated theories, requiring imagination, attention, education, and intellect, that better describe how learning works, are dismissed. Constructivist theories, flow theory, social learning theory, expectancy theory, perturbation theory, and other theories of behavior are mostly overlooked by the people who make decisions about schooling. These other theories are much more powerful predictors of human behavior than classical or operant conditioning, but they have been ignored because of their relative complexity. Although many educators engage in robust discussion around less brute educational practices, the application of conditioning wins out.

The Great Mistake

> "Fear of punishment has always been the great weapon of the teacher, and will always, of course, retain some place in the conditions of the schoolroom. The subject is so familiar that nothing more need be said about it."
>
> William James, *Talks To Teachers On Psychology*

Harvard psychologist and education philosopher, Edward Thorndike applied the ideas of behaviorism to education in the late 1800s, consequently influencing the next century of thinking and writing about teaching and learning. Although he understood that motivation was an important factor in learning, his experiments were done on animals, and the empirical evidence that came from his observations during these experiments helped him to generate his *Law of Effect*, which holds that people are motivated to change their behavior (i.e., learn) by being rewarded or punished. And, though behaviorism is superficially accurate with animals and with basic human behavior—mostly physical behaviors—the theory does not account for other more subtle and ubiquitous factors that affect what we do. Some of these factors include the difference between what helps people change their physical behavior and their cognitive behavior. For example, some people with disabilities like blindness, deafness, and major brain damage have overcome these types of disabilities and surpassed the abilities of those who are not blind, deaf, or have had a stroke. Rotter's (1966) *locus of control theory*, Dweck's (2008) *growth mindset theory*, Hogarth's (2001) *intuition theory*, and Brophy & Good's (1974) *expectancy theory* are more subtle, yes, but are also more powerful, influential, and applicable to academic learning, deep learning, and complex cognitive functioning. Other factors that are ignored are the negative effects of overusing rewards and punishments, like how dependency and addiction can grow out of the overuse of rewards, but even more important to consider is how punishment leads to shame and trauma, which inhibits the development of trusting relationships and self-efficacy, both of which are critical to all learning that extends beyond the most basic functions and is especially critical to classroom teaching.

Reinforcers and punishers, when overused—and they often are—come between teachers and students. This happens when we use incentives and punishments to control our students, interjecting our authority into those relationships. This leads to the frequent, often subtle, but sometimes less than subtle, abuse of power. When we abuse our power, our students learn not to trust us and may distrust other teachers as well. They become inhibited in their responses to us, afraid to take risks in their thinking, and conservative about their goals for achievement. They also become resentful and may feel betrayed.

Thorndike's description of the relation between reinforcers and punishers was also ultimately incomplete, but that did not stop his theories from becoming the foundation for well-regarded Harvard psychologist B.F. Skinner to champion behaviorist theories popularizing free will and overshadowing the important work of contemporaries like Harvard psychologists Albert Bandura, Jerome Bruner, Erik Erikson, University of Chicago psychologist Carl Rogers, and Brazilian philosopher Paulo Freire, whose theories of learning are more advanced and more powerful but also less easily understood and far less culturally and/or politically popular.

Thorndike's *law of effect* states that human responses when producing a desired effect are more likely to occur again. Conversely, responses that cause an unpleasant effect are less likely to happen again. The descriptions, desired effect, and unpleasant effect are what we call reinforcers and punishers today. Thorndike's theory of *the law of effect* has influenced classroom teaching so deeply that praising and ignoring behaviors have become synonymous with traditional teaching. Praise is so often used in classrooms to encourage and support skill attainment that teachers who do not use what has popularly been repackaged as *positive reinforcement* are accused of educational malpractice. Although praise has been shown in many studies to increase correct responses and appropriate behavior in classrooms, what is not considered is what happens when the student must perform the task outside of the classroom, where there is no certainty of praise.

Also not considered is the fact that praise disregards the need for internalizing, assimilating, and personalizing skill attainment so that it will be sustainable, meaningful, and practical for the learner beyond the classroom setting. And, though planned ignoring, the theory that the removal of an unconscious reinforcer, one that maintains unwanted behavior, has been shown in experiments to decrease the occurrence of some target behaviors under some circumstances, is more frequently an impractical tactic for classroom teaching because the original paradigm under which behaviorists conceived this method of behavior they called "extinction" assumed that there is one adult and one child in the dynamic, like a parent and child. Psychologists who promote planned ignoring were not conducting their experiments with groups of

30 children and one adult, as classrooms are often set up. The conclusions of those experiments that we so heavily lean on in our thinking about teaching and learning were conducted with one adult and one child. Planned ignoring has become one of behaviorism's silver bullets for education problem-solving, as promoted by Thorndike. An example would be that if a teacher intentionally did not pay attention to a student who was what we might call "whining," the student would supposedly realize that whining is not an effective way to get the teacher's attention and stop whining.

Of course, this example does not account for the situation where the whining behavior of one student sets a model for other students, especially when it is ignored by the teacher. The other students might assume that if the teacher is ignoring the whining, the teacher condones the behavior. Or, if the other students cannot tolerate whining as the teacher "ignores" it, they may reinforce the whining independent of the teacher by saying something like, "Dude! What the hell are you doing? That whining is annoying. Stop it! You sound like a baby."

Such a comment may, of course, also elicit a response from the whiner or from others, any of which may be disruptive to the learning process. In addition, the whining may be the student's way of communicating the existence of an unmet basic human need. Such a need, as mentioned, according to Maslow's *needs theory*, must be met for learning to take place. If the unmet need were fulfilled, it could be beneficial to the student's learning process, deepening that student-teacher relationship. But ignoring the signal for such a need, the whining, will not help our relationship with that student, and may, through transference, unconsciously remind the student of other adults, like his or her parents, who also ignore their needs, leading to an unnecessarily negative and unconscious psychodynamic condition.

This is an example where context and circumstances matter, which is why behaviorism is too simplistic to be applied to the classroom setting. It simply does not, is not, and often can't account for the myriad of circumstances that occur in the classroom setting. Yet, teacher training of all kinds and at all levels promotes behaviorist methods, not merely as one of many tools in the box but as the only tool for classroom management, problematic behavior, and even academic instruction. These ideas lead beginning teachers to believe that such a formulaic methodology is the foundation of their life's work with children. This reductionist approach to teaching relegates the profession to mechanistic A + B = C thinking. As alluring as this simplistic approach to teaching is, it is not only ineffective but irresponsible. It is also dangerous. Maslow said it best in his 1962 book, *The Psychology of Being*: "If all you have is a hammer, everything looks like a nail." Similarly, philosopher Abraham Kaplan wrote in his 1964 book, *The Conduct of Inquiry: Methodology for Behavioral Science*, about what he called the law of the instrument, saying, "Give a small boy a hammer, and he will find that everything he encounters needs pounding."

This is no less a case of confirmation bias run amuck within the modern tradition of schooling. An ancient proverb says, "With limited tools, single-minded people apply them inappropriately or indiscriminately." For the training of dogs, cats, or rats in laboratory settings, behaviorism does seem to work, especially if we continue to have low expectations of the emotional intelligence of such animals. Even for basic human skills, it can be effective in a one-on-one relationship, especially when parents are teaching their young children's basic skills, as long as the parents can punish and reward their child continuously. For classroom teachers, however, planned ignoring has not been shown to be an effective strategy. Yet this has not stopped education consultants, teacher educators, and school administrators from promoting it as a sound method for classroom *management*. In fact, because it often enhances a power dynamic where the teacher is in control, it is often overused, leading to and promoting both the use of fear and force in teaching. Ultimately, classical conditioning is, plain and simple, a type of force. And using force is not the best way to teach. In the very last book he wrote, *The Farther Reaches of Human Nature* (1971), Maslow repudiated the role of behaviorism as a means for educating human beings. He wrote:

> I could not stomach it anymore. It was impossible. Having a second baby and learning how profoundly different people are even before birth, made it impossible for me to think in terms of the kind of learning psychology in which one can teach anybody anything. Or the John B. Watson theory of "Give me two babies and I will make one into this and one into the other." It is as if he never had any children. We know only too well that a parent cannot make his children into anything. Children make themselves into something. The best we can do and frequently the most effect we can have is by serving as something to react against if the child presses too hard. (p.169)

Maslow rejected the application of objectivistic standardization in education. He decried the fact that social scientists had wrongly appropriated from various fields of science (like chemistry, biology, and physics) their investigation of non-human phenomena to create their own model for studying human behavior. He called this "the great mistake," and he exclaimed that since scientific fields such as chemistry, physics, and astronomy in their purest forms have no end and are value-free. Possessing knowledge of these subjects is an ends in and of itself and can have corollary applications. However, the study of human beings and the application of that study is far more complex than the study of stars, motion, and of matter. People are not ends. And they ought not have ends imposed on them by applying scientific thinking to education systems.

A Final Thought

Thorndike's work was based on his contemporary, Watson's, methodological behaviorism. Watson rejected any methods that were introspective and sought only to understand behavior by measuring what could be observed. Skinner recognized but marginalized the role of emotion, belief, and other influences on cognition as potential variables in observable behavior because they are messy and require a complex and sophisticated approach to understanding human behavior and learning. What Watson, Skinner, Thorndike, Pavlov, and other behaviorists ignored is that people's personal beliefs and ideas about themselves and the world help them form their identities through uniquely and highly individualized stories about the self/world dynamic. And these stories influence their behavior in significant and important ways and, these beliefs cannot be observed in the laboratory or measured with quantitative techniques.

The Russian philosopher, Mikhail Bakhtin, discussed the concept of "internally persuasive discourse" in his writings about thinking and learning. His theory of *internally persuasive discourse* in humanism proves to be a confounding element for any theory of human behavior, especially behaviorism as it may apply to teaching. Bakhtin's theories of narrative discourse show us that fear is not merely a byproduct of force but is often a means of enhancing it. We often unknowingly create an "authoritative discourse" when force is used as a tool to control students. Manipulating students' fears of failure, disapproval and punishment has been integral to the use of force in schools, yet it is not only ineffective but also dangerous.

Alternatively, we may consider Maslow's theory regarding the *awakening of B-values?* Also, in his *The Farther Reaches of Human Nature*, Maslow wrote about "being-cognition" (also described as "B-cognition" or "B-values"), which he explained in relation to "deficiency-cognition" (or "D-cognition"), as reaching "beyond polarities ... to see the underlying oneness," integrating everything into a comprehensive whole. He wrote in his *theory of B-values*, "People would be stronger, healthier, and would take their own lives into their hands to a greater extent." B-values include the traits: truth: honesty, reality, richness, beauty, completeness, justice, benevolence, aliveness, perfection, uniqueness, wholeness, unity, integration, interconnectedness, organization, structure, dichotomy-transcendence, order, process, spontaneity, self-regulation, idiosyncrasy; individuality, non-comparability, novelty, suitability, fulfillment, abstractness, and richness: differentiation, complexity, intricacy, independence, self-determination, separateness, effortlessness, grace, playfulness, fun, amusement, humor, autonomy, and joy. The values that schools will have for students in 2024 are not at all like Maslow's. I will call these values schools hold for students today our *F-values* (force values). They are: compliance, conformity, normality, convention, non-resistance, willingness, servility, civility, tradition, fashion, manageability, passivity, duty, differentially, subordination, subservience, dependence, comparable, submissiveness, and obedience.

Can schools hold both F-values and B-values simultaneously?

American feminist, educator, and philosopher, Nel Noddings, in her *Caring: A Feminist Approach to Ethics and Moral Education*, wrote, "[The teacher] does not need to resort to punishment, because the rules are not sacred to her." To Noddings, the student's welfare was sacred, not *the rules*. Noddings (1999) believed strongly that education systems must embrace an ethic of care where the relationship between student and teacher becomes our primary concern, discussing that as we respond to our students' needs, we can see the need for the most differentiated curriculum and that as we work closely with students, we will be moved by our students' distinct needs and interests. Our claims to care about our students must be based on our long-term interest in their welfare and not on our attempts to control them.

· 4 ·

INTRINSIC MOTIVATION

"The personal fears that students and teachers bring to the classroom are fed by the fact that the roots of education are sunk deep in fearful ground."

Parker Palmer, The Courage To Teach

To say that our use of force is disruptive to our relationship with students is an absolute understatement. Our overpowering and overwhelming use of personal, positional, psychological, and societal force, backed by systems of adult power, has the potential to annihilate trust, decimate any common understanding we have with our students, and silence identity. Forceful adult behavior can easily stop *intrinsic motivation* in its tracks, requiring a teacher to employ techniques aligned with extrinsic motivation like bribery and punishment just to get through a lesson. And *extrinsic motivation*, including negative reinforcement like withholding approval, only further alienates our students.

According to motivation experts, Richard Ryan and Edward Deci (2017), *intrinsic motivation* is what moves us to engage in a task or set of tasks because we find them personally rewarding, interesting, and stimulating. With *intrinsic motivation*, we perform an activity for its own sake, not because we desire a reward that is separate from the activity itself. The behavior itself is the reward. Conversely, *extrinsic motivation* works by engaging us in an activity because we desire a reward or want to avoid something painful. We initiate such behavior not for enjoyment, stimulation, or curiosity, but because we find it satisfying. We do it because of our expectation of a desirable and assumed outcome or because we want to avoid something painful, fearful, or unpleasant.

Education in American schools is almost entirely based on extrinsic motivation, which is naturally coercive. For too long, teaching has been about force, has used force, and has been forceful. Schools, K-12 through higher education, have been pushing students toward academic outcomes based on established cultural norms, even though this is not the most effective way to help people learn, and many of the cultural norms we used to build those outcomes are now irrelevant. Ryan, Deci, and their colleague, Wendy Grolnick's, research on motivation (2017, 2007, & 1986) shows that classical and operant conditioning, the use of punishments and rewards to change human behavior, have only short-term effects compared to more humanistic models that are based on *intrinsic motivation* like *self-actualization* and holistic explorations of internal loci of control.

Instead of "laying down the law" or, as Noddings warns "holding the rules sacred" when students "get out of line," teachers may do well to situate themselves in a position of curiosity about what is happening rather than trying to hold onto or recapture control. Harvard psychologist and researcher, Ellen Langer (2016), has also published significant research on *mindfulness in education*, exposing the limits of using *extrinsic motivation* in teaching as well as the potential benefits of embracing approaches that stimulate *intrinsic motivation*.

Bakhtin (2010 & 1981) discussed at length the social voices we choose to speak through, and it is within our power to use nuance as we employ our authoritative voices with our students. Bakhtin's analysis of discourses is especially relevant to how we enter into dialogues with our students because it is how we embody language through our loudness, facial expressions, and how we pose our whole frames. Language itself is quite forceful, but it is rarely divorced from how we express our approval, disapproval, respect, and irritation.

Too often, our behavior, our tone of voice, our body language, and the decisions we make reflect our needs instead of theirs. For example, we may be unconscious of our need to maintain control of our classroom environment at a certain level. We may feel as if we need to make progress in covering the curriculum. Most of us feel as if we need to make a good impression on our bosses and colleagues, at least in the first few years. These are the tips of a very large iceberg, representing our perceived personal needs as teachers. When we put our needs above our students' needs, they sense it. And they resent it. Even if we are "there for them" in large part, more than not, our students often interpret our attention to our own needs as an indifference to theirs. This is especially true when our needs conflict with theirs. Deci (2004) writes in his article on *intrinsic motivation* and self-determination for the *Encyclopedia of Applied Psychology*, "Because controlling methods have been related to poorer conceptual learning, poorer performance on problem-solving tasks, less creativity, and lower feelings of self-worth, the evidence is compelling that more autonomy-supportive approaches in classrooms have substantial advantages for learning, performance, and development."

Wu Wei

"People in Wu Wei feel as if they are doing nothing, while at the same time they might be creating a brilliant work of art, smoothly negotiating a complex social situation, or even bringing the entire world into harmonious order."

Edward Slingerland, *Trying not to Try: The Art and Science of Spontaneity*

What I did not understand when I first started teaching was that people are not easily coerced. Even children can spot our attempts to manipulate them using basic carrots and sticks, and they then resist us. After they have built up the wall of habitual resistance, it's almost impossible for them to take it down. So, what do we do? How do teachers get students to do things they don't want to? Things that are good for them? Things they need, like literacy and critical thinking skills, writing skills, and numeracy skills are often forced upon children, because their teachers do not know any other way to teach them.

The first problem is one that we, the teachers, create. It isn't always there until after we make it. And that is the presumption that learning to read, do math, and develop other academic skills are things children do not want to do. That's not necessarily true. What is true is that they don't want to learn these things the way we teach them. That, I do know. The answer is in the ancient Chinese teachings of the Master, Lao Tzu. He was the founder of Taoism and author of the *Tao Te Ching*, and he believed that when people are in harmony with the Tao (the intuitive knowing of experience that cannot be understood, only lived), they behave in a natural, unforced way. Lao Tzu mastered the spiritual practice of a purely natural way of being, like the way planets revolve around the sun, glaciers recede, plants bend toward the sun, and fires burn oxygen. He called this *Wu Wei*.

Wu Wei is defined as the ancient Chinese art of doing nothing by accomplishing through being—not through effort. In stark contrast to the behaviorist theories of motivation, with Wu Wei, we do not need incentives, punishments, or even a purpose for acting. We do things, because we feel fulfilled, extremely alive, and whole in that experience, not for an external outcome or to accomplish a goal someone else sets for us. There is a feeling associated with Wu Wei, and that is what noted motivation expert and University of Chicago psychologist, Mihalyi Csikszentmihalyi (1990) called *flow*.

Like B-Cognitionn,this is the feeling of absolute immersion in experience. A person in flow is so engrossed in an activity that their worries, sense of time, self-consciousness, and need for ego gratification fade away. The person completes the task because they are drawn into it, are curious, and are magnetically captivated by the experience because it provides the right level of challenge for them. It places them in the present moment, where the future and past do not distract them. Csikszentmihalyi linked the flow state to a euphoric sensation, and he referred to experiences that became identified as "flow experiences" as peak or optimal experiences. Nobel Prize-winning scientists, elite surgeons, professional athletes, virtuoso musicians, and other individuals who perform at extremely high levels are familiar with this state of being. Csikszentmihalyi's (2014) research on motivation shows that flow leads to the deepest kinds of learning, enhances students' interest in what school has to offer, and eliminates the need to punish or reward students for their behavior. Today's classrooms are challenging places to create flow because of schools' overemphasis on outcomes. Csikszentmihalyi's research also shows that it is the very act of being attached to outcomes that diminishes intrinsic motivation. In his book, *Trying Not to Try: The Art and Science of Spontaneity*, philosopher, professor, and author, Edward Slingerland (2015) explains that it is our investment in *processes rather than products* that allow for Wu Wei. However, there are a few things that teachers can try to stimulate Wu Wei and flow.

1. *Find the right balance between challenge and ease*. According to Csikszentmihalyi (1975 & 1990), to be "in flow," an activity must be inherently challenging. But, as noted Soviet psychologist Lev Vygotsky's (1980) developmental theory of the "Zone of Proximal Development" posits, it need not be more difficult than one level beyond the student's ability. If there is too much difficulty, students will experience the challenge as a threat and either outright resist or

casually avoid the activity. A task that is not challenging enough will bore the students, and that lack of interest is a liability to the learning process. In both cases, it is not possible for the teacher to find the right level of challenge—the right fit—without first knowing what your students can and cannot do, without knowing them as people, or without understanding their interests and personalities, making trust and relationships extremely important for teaching.

2. *Learning activities must have some aspect that students think intersects with their lives.* Education researcher, Tim Seifert (2004) conducted research on motivation in schools which showed that when students think of a lesson as relevant to their lives, they are more likely to engage in it. This requires teachers to know their students, which also requires them to have relationships with them. If students don't think the lesson matters, in as far as their own lives are concerned, they will not experience the flow state and will not be intrinsically motivated.

3. *Prioritize Choice.* Numerous studies show (Allen et al., 1994; Deci & Flaste, 1995; Deci & Ryan, 1987; Grolnik & Ryan, 1987) that when students are given the autonomy that allows them to choose their own learning activities, they start working sooner and keep working beyond what they normally otherwise would. This is because they do not think of the activity they chose as work, and they are more likely to view the task as *play* instead. A person in flow loses track of time and has increased attention, concentration, and focus. More importantly, their performance is enhanced.

4. *Include students in classroom goal-setting.* By doing so, students will be more likely to accept the feedback that teachers provide. Teachers often provide feedback that is ignored by students, and then we might wonder why we wasted our time giving it, but students are less likely to ignore feedback when it relates to a performance task that they are interested in, that they chose, and for which they ultimately set the goal. Csikszentmihalyi has explained that flow activities often have clear goals, providing structure and direction. In the classroom, when students help to create their own goals, they are more likely to monitor their own progress toward achieving them. Deci & Ryan's (1985) research and Csikszentmihalyi's (1997) study on flow theory show that when students receive regular and consistent feedback during the process of completing a learning activity, they are more likely to remain engaged in it.

5. *Building relationships with students can't be overlooked.* As explained in numbers 1 and 2 above, without knowing our students as people, without understanding their interests, their lives, and their personalities, it is very hard to match the level of help we should give them. And this is just one reason why building relationships is important. Education researchers Carol Ann Tomlinson and Kristina Doubet (2005) explain that positive student-teacher relationships have the potential to enhance connections and improve performance. Although it takes time to build relationships with students, the payoff is often significant. Abuhamdeh and Csikszentmihalyi's (2012) work on attention confirmed that interpersonal relationships are a powerful way to increase student performance through stimulating intrinsic motivation. So, getting to know our students is the first step. This requires us to show them who we are as well. If we have rapport with our students, they are more likely to ask us questions and express their interests. When they ask us questions and express their interests, we are better able to help them succeed.

6. *Experiential learning is important.* If the classroom is not filled with hands-on learning activities, projects, and experiences, children either never reach the flow state or drop out of it, becoming passive learners. Student-centered problem-based learning activities are more likely to maintain flow in the classroom once it has been achieved than any teacher-centered method. Unlike lecturing or teacher-led class discussions that are not student-centered, Wu Wei requires us to be less in control of their learning experience. We must work less, understanding that performance is the responsibility of students. John Dewey, Paulo Freire, Lev Vygotsky, Jerome Bruner, Albert Bandura, Kurt Lewin, Jean-Paul Piaget, David Kolb, Peter Senge, Carl Rogers, Maria Montessori, and many other thinkers from sociology, economics, psychology, and education have agreed for decades about the necessity for students to have direct experience and immersion in the realities for which they are learning. For a person to apply academic learning to real-life situations, their knowledge must move from abstract, classroom-based conceptions to concrete experience.

Experience cannot be a substitute for theoretical knowledge because motivation depends on our grounding of theoretical knowledge in personal experience. Without intrinsic motivation and internalizing the schema that make up the building blocks of both simple and complex knowledge of academic skills, some level of coercion, perhaps through an accountability scheme, seems to be required. *Wu Wei* is the opposite of force, and the inherent beauty of Wu Wei is that its ease of automation makes the desire for control that our pedagogical tradition goads us into thinking necessary for teaching and learning, the same one that interferes with deep and personal learning, unnecessary. The irony is that most of our problems in education can be solved by doing less instead of more.

A Final Thought

The practice of Wu Wei and the effort to seek flow are inherently opposed to the use of force and fear. Where teachers often use various methods of force to try to coerce learning, these methods work counter to our purpose as educators. Instead, we must let go of our own fears of losing the illusory control that we pretend to have and instead release our idea of it. That is where we can create space for learning to happen, rather than trying to force it into existence.

· 5 ·

THE COMPLIANCE-BASED MODEL

> We discovered that education is not something which the teacher does, but that it is a natural process which develops spontaneously in the human being.
>
> Maria Montessori, *The Absorbent Mind*

At one point in my career as a classroom teacher, I realized that I did not believe in the compliance-based model of teaching, so I had to let that way of doing business go. I came to understand that I did not think it was a good way, a practical way, or even an efficient way of teaching. I didn't arrive at this conclusion without confronting my fears and letting go of my deeply held need for control that was programmed deep in this teacher's operating system.

I had to face the fact that I was going to go my own way, abandoning the dominant compliance-based model, alone and unsupported. I felt lost and untethered at first. I did not have any guidance, collaborators, or models, but as I worked to build relationships with my students and a few colleagues who tolerated my vision, I found that *using as little force as necessary* was better than what I had been doing. Teachers are generally unsupported in American schools unless we are lucky enough to have a boss or colleague who has the time and desire to commit to helping us. Unfortunately, most administrators don't even have the energy or capacity to do their own jobs, never mind helping teachers do ours. Working at a school can be overwhelming. When I started out, I was afraid to ask for help. I thought it was a sign of weakness, but after realizing that I was not reaching my students and out of desperation, I learned to ask my bosses, colleagues, and even my students for help when I needed it. And, just often enough, sometimes one or the other would help me. More importantly than whether their advice was useful, simply getting some advice helped me feel less alone.

Pain is a fact of life. Accepting that we don't have control over everything may help us avoid needless suffering, but it won't stop the pain. I have learned to make use of the pain by seeing it as an opportunity to teach me what I need to know at any given moment. I learned to fear criticism less when I stopped listening to it, whether it came from inside me or from someone else. The less I listened to it, the less often people criticized me. Nonetheless, going it on my own was painful, lonely, and scary.

One day, a student criticized me for not accomplishing all the things I planned to do in a particular lesson. I had gotten off topic that day—a tangent that was educational and pertinent but perhaps not prudent and defied the normal focused teaching she had come to expect from traditional instruction. Just before the bell rang, she said to a classmate, loudly enough for me to hear, "If he had stuck to the agenda, he would have covered everything."

Although I didn't ignore her, since she wasn't talking to me, I also didn't respond to her. But her classmate did respond, watching me for a reaction. "He doesn't seem to care what you think," he said, which wasn't entirely true. But I was silently trying to follow the advice of author and medical doctor, Don Miguel Ruiz from his book *The Four Agreements*. His second agreement says: *Don't take anything personally*. The second agreement has given me a method for dealing with people who might get under my skin and can press my buttons.

Pressing my buttons doesn't work well anymore because I have a strong enough sense of self-efficacy to ignore most criticism that I can't use and didn't ask for. In the course of my career as a teacher, I have learned that if I rely on others' opinions of my teaching to prop up my self-confidence, when their feedback turns to criticism, it can be painful because I allow it to sink deep within me, often arousing doubt instead of reflection. Self-confidence is essential for teachers. In many other jobs, an insecure person might be able to survive for a week, a month, or perhaps even longer, but in teaching, self-doubt is toxic. Teachers with significant self-doubt don't last more than a day or two. So, I have worked on fortifying my self-confidence and my sense of identity by understanding, knowing, and accepting who I am and loving who I am. Sometimes, even today, a person will criticize me, and it irritates me, which shows I still have some work to do in this area. Pain shows us when we have the opportunity to do that work, and as teachers, it is critical that we not delay in doing it because ours is an interpersonal vocation. It's even more important, though, as imperfect as we are, to believe in ourselves, accept ourselves, and love ourselves. Daily, teaching is a careful balance between having the raw courage to be reflective, self-effacing, and composed without losing faith and falling off the cliff into a sea of self-doubt at the mercy of the storm.

Ruiz's second agreement also helped me understand that each individual person has their own worldview, altering the perceptions that regulate their beliefs and behavior. Ruiz explains that people's criticisms of us are actually projections of their own personal reality. He believes that feelings like jealousy, envy, anger, inadequacy, and sadness will disappear once we stop taking things personally. Fear goes hand in hand with taking things personally. If we fear what others think of us, it is because we either have never taken a good look at who we are and we fear that we won't like what we see if we do, or we have taken a look and don't think much of ourselves. Usually, if we don't like what we see, we need to look closer, either to examine what we can do to be a person we can love or because we stopped looking too early and only saw what we were taught to see at a very young age by people who did not honor our humanity. It is important for teachers to have the courage to love themselves because we are consistently and unconsciously modeling the way we treat ourselves in front of our students. If we love ourselves, they will see that. If we doubt ourselves, they see that. When we lose faith, they know. They do not miss much. And, even when they do not consciously know what is going on with us, they sense it.

When I was still a young teacher, much of my fear rose out of my lack of understanding, lack of background, and lack of knowledge about curriculum. It seemed like a puzzle to me, one for which I could not see the point entirely. There was and still is so much more emphasis on curriculum than is necessary. I am not arguing against it. Curriculum is important, but the answer to the puzzle wasn't about my ignorance. It was and still is about the absolute overemphasis on curriculum. It still feels more like packaging to me than the substance of the thing. And, now that academia is my professional home, I have more foundational knowledge of curriculum theory and, therefore, enough perspective to know that I was making too much of it because the teaching profession does. Now, I see that some "children" like to play with the box more than what is inside it.

Long before I explicitly understood that curriculum has over the past four decades become a superstructure, supporting an outdated, ever-faltering, and inherently flawed model of education that is increasingly based on and for adult control, political power, and economic purposes, I learned to let go of the obsession with curriculum that I had inherited from the system that educated me. I had to, so I could embrace my growing belief that teaching requires an "ethic of care" that puts my students' humanity first and everything else after that, including curriculum and subject matter knowledge. I also had to accept that I had little control over my students' cognitive growth—never mind academic outcomes, high-stakes testing, or cultural literacy. It was with this new focus that I found my way to a place where my students were successful as learners without any need for the heavy-handed tactics of *education as domestication*. Because whether we dress them up with catchy academic names like "transferability of skills," "implementing inclusionary practices," or "optimal delivery approaches," they are all at heart autocratic teaching models.

I came to understand that teaching the curriculum is a waste of time if I don't care about who I teach it to. And I figured out that if my students sensed (and they did) that I cared more about reading and writing skills than about them, they would not be able to engage me in reading and writing activities, no matter how many best practices I used, no matter how much I knew about ELA, and no matter how rigorous my lessons were. Letting go of my fear that I was not focused enough on the curriculum sometimes meant letting go of the curriculum itself, and I won't apologize for that.

As I said before, I used to be afraid that my colleagues didn't respect me as a teacher, until I realized two things: first, most of them, like me, don't know what teaching even is, and second, that other people's respect for us is no replacement for our own self-respect. The fact that I feared that my students would find me boring, stupid, or foolish makes me smile now, because I am now absolutely sure that I am boring, stupid, and foolish to some people, and there is very little I can do about it. If I can improve, I will. But, the more open, honest, authentic, vulnerable, and imperfect I am with my students, the less they think I'm boring. That fear, like my other fears, didn't prevent me from being boring, stupid, or foolish. It actually catalyzed those qualities into reality, because I had reacted to things by pretending to be perfect, omnipotent, and infallible, which are inherently stupid and foolish, if not boring too. Fear makes us do stupid things. As I noted previously, German philosopher Friedrich Nietzsche, wrote in his 1886 book *Beyond Good and Evil: Prelude to a Philosophy of the Future*, "Beware that, when fighting monsters, you yourself do not become a monster... for when you gaze long into the abyss. The abyss gazes also into you."

We force ourselves to act as someone we are not only out of fear. But being our imperfectly ignorant selves, vulnerable, and exposed in front of our students is both more compelling and, at the same time, totally disarming, inviting them to be open, trusting, and being themselves. Once I stopped pretending to be someone else, I never had a problem where students would talk over me again, because it turns out that the imperfect me, the vulnerable, ignorant, and youthfully curious John Brown, is interesting, and they want to hear the crazy shit I have to say. I rarely ever hold back anymore. I tell the truth as I know it, as strange, unpopular, unconventional, uncool, unproven, and uncomfortable as it may be, and there is nothing more interesting than someone's unvarnished truth.

Embracing the Tension of Teaching

A method of instruction should have the objective of leading the child to discover for himself. Telling children and then testing them on what they have been told inevitably has the effect of producing bench-bound learners whose motivation for learning is likely to be extrinsic to the task—pleasing the teacher, getting into college, artificially maintaining self-esteem. As Bruner writes (1979) "the virtues of encouraging discovery are of two kinds. In the first place, the child will make what he learns his own and will fit his discovery into the interior world of cultures that he creates for himself. Discovery and the sense of confidence it provides are the proper rewards for learning."

My truth is undeniable, and so is theirs. Like thunder or the sun pouring through the clouds after a storm, like birth or death, the truth, yours or mine, mine or my students', can't be negated. My truth can be rejected by someone else or disowned by me, but only fools pretend they don't hear a clap of thunder. When my truth and their truth contradict one another, when one of my students holds something to be true and I hold an opposing truth, there is tension. This tension is common, and I used to reject their truth, thinking that that tension was dangerous and a threat to my position. Such a rejection is an unnecessary use of force, leading only to resentment and something much worse than tension: animosity. The tension between my truth and their truth is, in fact, not dangerous. It is not antithetical to teaching or learning. That tension is real. I do not fear it anymore. That tension is useful and important, and when it is released, its energy fuels epiphany, inspiration, and identity. Threat to my position? What position did I think I was defending, anyway?

This is why I have embraced that tension. I honor their truth now, whether it matches mine, contradicts it, or stands in simple contrast to it. Embedded in my relationship with my students is what Bakhtin (1981 & 2010) called the *sacred dialogic tension* between these opposing truths. My mentor and friend, Bob Cunningham, calls this "resolute awareness." It can only be experienced in the present moment. Unlike soldiers, who must not show fear in the face of conflict, as teachers, we must do the opposite and stand vulnerable before our students, laying ourselves bare and exposing our ignorance, authentic, unguarded, and totally assailable even by a single, perhaps unreasonable student's opinion. We must leave ourselves utterly embarrassed before a whole class of students by being publicly excoriated. This is a most unfortunate necessity for the opening of *dialogical spaces* where authentic learning occurs. In a world filled with chaos, oppression, brutal authority, and continuous attempts by people to win control, regain it, or maintain it, we must not inflate our positions to protect the illusion that our egos project as truth.

The exercise of power and control is quick, unapologetic, and overwhelming for us and for our students, and it's not something we need more of it in schools. We need less of it. Counterintuitively, it is my experience that the most powerful teaching dynamics are those where the teacher possesses power but does not exercise it when called out, challenged, or even baited by students. The teacher who remains *resolutely aware* of the authority in their self-possession, remains dedicated to the acceptance of a nonviolent tension held in the present moment, watches more than acts, invests in being more than in doing, and resolves to feel the moment while still thinking about their feelings is a true pedagogue.

For in moments like these, where an honest dialogic discourse between students and teachers exists, there is the opportunity for new growth of understanding, the construction of new knowledge, the expansion of consciousness, and the deepening of our capacity for teachers as students and students as teachers. Shared because of the seemingly impossibility of the absolutely and obviously possible dialogical space, this is more than representational. It is reality. And, because it is always novel and always shared, because we are always vulnerable, taking the risk to be weak and wrong and scared and defeated, this courage is nothing less than pure epiphany.

Dr. Martin Luther King Jr. (1963) believed that such tension was part of the learning process. "I have earnestly opposed violent tension, but there is a type of constructive, nonviolent tension which is necessary for growth." Brazilian philosopher, educator, and author, in his seminal 1968 book, *Pedagogy of the*

Oppressed, described tension as necessary and productive for the attainment of new knowledge. Bakhtin (1981 & 1986) argued that our understanding of our students and their understanding of us, constructed in language, is reflexive, continual, and as transactional as it is transformational. The expression of meaning without response belies the construction of knowledge. It is within interaction and through struggling with our thoughts and ideas, as well as the thoughts and ideas of other people that meaningful cognition occurs. This shared understanding is the root of learning.

As a professor of education, one of my responsibilities is to observe student teaching practicums for the purposes of coaching preservice and new teachers and to evaluate their abilities as teachers, so I visit many classrooms, see many interactions between students and teachers, and often see the interactions of the mentors assigned to the preservice and new teachers. During these visits, over the past 10 years, in 30 different schools, I have seen something that should be strange but is, in fact, quite ordinary.

I have been watching teachers simply give their students directions and then grade them on how well those students followed their directions. They think they are teaching. When I was a high school teacher, I witnessed this as well, and I also see it at the university. This is not particularly offensive or criminal. I'll admit I have done it myself, still do it, and I have lied to myself too, that it was teaching. But it is not. Giving students assignments and then grading them on how well they followed the rubric, the grading criteria, and the course expectations is not teaching. I know that compliance-based education has its tentacles deep in the belief systems of many individual teachers and all levels of education, myself included. In fact, because my evaluators at the university are still more concerned with whether or not my syllabi have rubrics than if my students are learning, my syllabi are too long, too prescriptive, and too focused on compliance. Giving directions and evaluating people based on how well they follow them is not about learning. It is about power. Our idea of "curriculum" is fraught with forcefulness and bound to draw resistance, resentment, and/or passivity from anybody. And 21st-century adolescents, especially, are not buying it.

Requiring compliance from young people in schools is rooted in a tradition of treating people like things and using them as means to our ends. Maslow declared back in 1971 that this model of teaching has been a "great mistake."

The great mistake that we are now learning about is that this model, which developed from a study of objects and of things, has been illegitimately used for the study of human beings. It is a terrible technique. It has not worked."
The farther reaches of human nature

Maslow understood that the objectives-based system of education did not work in 1971. Regrettably, 50 years later, we are not treating students more like human beings than things. In fact, we are treating them even more like objects than we ever have before. We are more concerned with our continually shifting adult results, ends, goals, objectives, and outcomes than we are with them. When will we see that we are wrong here? When will we learn this lesson? When will we admit that an outcome has become little more than a payday?

A Final Thought

Only one action is more powerful, more impressive, more sustainable, and more seductive than using one's authority to act forcefully, controlling outcomes and other people, and that is the simple act of surrender. As a teacher, I learned that my power could come from my students instead of something I had to draw from institutions. The tradition and interpersonal strategy used to control students are less powerful than one simple moment of surrender. I had to make myself vulnerable to my students within the context of my humanity first, and trust that:

1. They would not annihilate me, and
2. That if they tried to annihilate me (for who would blame them), I would survive and persevere.

This was a risk, but it ultimately worked and has worked again and again. I trusted them, and they did not reduce me to nothing. In fact, my trust was rewarded. They began to trust me, which increased our sense of relationship, our connectedness, and our collective power to experience a shared understanding of reality, a shared yet sometimes contested consciousness of truth. This is the risk every good teacher takes.

· 6 ·

WHAT IS PEDAGOGY?

Recently, a student asked me how I would define the word "pedagogy," and in that moment, I decided that I could not adequately define such a word on the spot. I told her I would get back to her, and now here is my reply.

More frequently used than pedagogy, the word *pedagogue* is used today to describe a strict, pedantic, and demanding instructor. The ancient Greek word, παιδαγωγός or paidagōgos, etymologically had a very different connotation. The "paidagog" of Plato's time was an adult who, in servitude and with great care, literally *walked* children to school each day. In ancient times, the word was taken to mean the one who guides, protects, or leads. That pedagogy seems gentler than the associations the word conjures up nowadays.

However, the idea of pedagogy is much more complex than either of these. In contemporary discourse, the word pedagogy is sometimes used to describe learning theory and other times to describe the practice of such theory. It has become an example of academic language, referring to the exploration of how knowledge and skill grow as facilitated within the context of another person or other people (i.e., students and teachers). When curriculum structuralists explain the meaning of pedagogy, they use the word transfer instead of the word grow. Since I'm no curriculum structuralist, I use the word grow.

There are various pedagogies described throughout the history of educational thought. For example, the ancient Greek philosopher Socrates believed that his students ought to think for themselves and interact with them, asking them questions, debating points, and literally arguing with them to inspire independent thought in them. His pedagogy stands in stark contrast to that of Edward Thorndike, who described teaching as an act that requires the conditioning of student behavior through punishments and rewards. Lev Vygotsky, believed that the role of the teacher is to mediate students' ability to cognitively construct their own conceptions of the world rather than adopting the ideas of other people. This is just a small sample of the many different pedagogies that have been described over the past century.

At the heart of these and any other pedagogies is a theory of interaction. Such a theory describes the behaviors that individuals encounter during the learning process. Often, pedagogy is understood as a set of such behaviors that can be replicated, imitated, or repeated for the purposes of institutional or social normative objectives; however, this particular understanding is better described by the word *curriculum*.

Many distinct pedagogies have evolved over millennia, each reflecting historical, philosophical, political, biological, social, psychological, scientific, or personal stances. Many pedagogical theories include a paradigm of agency, where the roles of the learner and the teacher are defined and explained. For example, the role of teacher could be associated with coaching, or the role could be associated with modeling. There are, of course, many variations of the learner-teacher relationship, none of which is absolutely individualized, meaning most teachers use a blend of pedagogies when they interact with their students.

Hidden Pedagogy

Professional educators are guided by our own unique pedagogies, whether we are conscious of them or not. These theoretical frameworks of how learning works shape our instructional decisions and, therefore, our actions as they relate to how we interact with our students. Many of us are actually only vaguely aware of the pedagogies we enact, partially because the lines between various pedagogies are rarely clear and also because teacher education rarely addresses learning theory or pedagogy, but mostly because nearly all of us lack awareness of how deeply socialized we have become regarding our beliefs about how people learn.

In addition, a teacher's personal pedagogy is rarely fixed. Dynamic and constantly shaped by experience, like our learning theories, our pedagogies are constantly evolving, and such evolutions are not linear. Scholars Henry Giroux and Philip W. Jackson used the term "hidden curriculum" to describe the unconscious consequences of socialization and the domestication of young people through their families, religion, schools, and other cultural institutions that reinforce social norms. The hidden curriculum is a powerful concept, and for our purposes, I want to think aloud here about the hidden pedagogy. I am describing the phenomenon where "teachers," unquestioningly and without reflection, often unintentionally subsume the pedagogical belief system or systems that were used to educate them when they were students—from a very early age through adulthood. We adopt these means easily and naturally through repetition during the years of our lives when we are dependent and impressionable children.

The decision-making processes of teachers always influence the strategies, activities, expectations, and assignments that we employ in our teaching, whether we are unconscious of them or fully aware of them. And often, we are unaware of what learning theories we follow, despite any declarations we might make about learning theories we "believe in."

Learning Theory vs. Pedagogical Thinking

Unfortunately, since colleges of education and teacher PD prioritize teaching methodology over learning theory, many teachers lack a basic understanding of the various ideas about how people learn. This is why pedagogy is important for teachers to consider. Without terminology that we can use to identify the various aspects and ideas of about our teaching and and how they relate to the daily events that occur in our teaching, we cannot reflect, analyze, and discuss what we understand and believe about our behavior and the behavior of others. Without having a dialogue about interactions that are healthy, positive, and effective, as well as those that are destructive, corrosive, and misaligned with our values Any thoughts, feelings, or reflections we have about our roles as teachers or as students will be consumed in the vacuum created by expediency, tradition, and inertia.

If there seems to be no difference between learning theory and pedagogical thinking, that is because learning theory plays a central role in every teacher's role identification within the student-teacher relationship, but learning theory is distinct from pedagogical thinking. Our pedagogies are more complex than our learning theories because, although they subsume our beliefs about how people learn, they also include our personal understandings about authority, identity, personality, our personal histories as students and teachers, and our behavior patterns, which are governed by our conscious and unconscious thoughts and emotions.

Modes of pedagogical thinking

The scientific pedagogy, aligned with standards-based instruction, is the most conventional pedagogy at this time in the history of education policy and theory. It is primarily outcome-based, focusing on the defined and pre-ordained subject matter and standardized basic skills that adult decision-makers (not learners) want teachers to transfer to learners, employing instructional models that include the use of conditioning through incentives, coercion, manipulation, and other more forceful means used to achieve goals that were selected for the learner instead of by or with the learner. Based on the simple principles of mechanical engineering, scientific pedagogy is reductive and objectivist, relying on the assumption that teachers can and will accept that their students are simple, static objects that can be easily manipulated. Thorndike's theories are at the center of most outcome-based approaches to teaching. His "law of effect," his behaviorist paradigms, and his strong belief in human conditioning, similar to Ivan Pavlov's, John Watson's, and B.F. Skinner's, provided a framework for what seems like an orderly connection between curriculum and instruction. In 1949, Ralph Tyler, the American educator known for originating The National Assessment of Educational Progress (NAEP), was developing a new organization for school curricula, began honing his scientific pedagogical approach to teaching into a framework, and published a book about it titled *Principles of Curriculum and Instruction*.

Known as *The Tyler Rationale*, this book laid out a deceptively simple structure for delivering and measuring the effectiveness of instruction. Tyler believed that teachers should ask these questions before we begin:

- What educational purposes do we (adults in control) seek to attain? (i.e., learning objectives)
- What learning experiences are most useful in attaining these objectives? (i.e., learning activities)
- How can we organize these learning experiences to have the maximum effect possible? (i.e., efficacy)
- How will we evaluate the level of effectiveness of the chosen learning experiences to make sure we get to accomplish the objectives we want for our students? (i.e., assessment)

Although some curriculum experts, like *Understanding by design* (UBD) originators Jay McTighe and Grant Wiggins (2005), may describe the pedagogies that accompany this brand of curriculum as "student-centered," the fact that in their taxonomies, they employ terms like "transfer goals" demonstrates that the concepts they base their frameworks on are reliant on the teacher acting as an agent of the dominant culture, placing "the teacher-as-agent" at the center of the instructional interaction, not the student. After all, who chooses the objectives? And who chooses what is transferred; from whom is it transferred?

Well, it's not the students. That's for sure. And, nowadays, even teachers are often boxed out of instructional decisions. Tyler went on to work for the federal government as an advisor during the writing of the Elementary and Secondary Education Act of 1965. He also led the group that created the The National Assessment for Educational Progress or NAEP. His legacy, which we surrounds us in schools today, has shaped academic schooling into a rather technical and scientific endeavor. It is the most pervasive of all the pedagogies adolescents experience in public schools today.

The humanist pedagogy focuses on students' needs, backgrounds, and interests and claims to hold individual human freedoms as pre-eminent. This pedagogy is based on various developmental models from psychology, philosophy, sociology, and neurology. Teachers who are faithful to the humanist school prioritize the use of a holistic approach to instruction. Teachers who ascribe to the humanist approach rely heavily on a diversity of developmental theories, of which Maslow's *hierarchy of needs* and Bandura's *theories of self-efficacy* and *triadic reciprocal determinism* top the list. And, although John Dewey is most notably associated with pragmatist pedagogies, his strong belief in the autonomy of the learner influenced humanist psychologists like Carl Rogers, who, unlike Thorndike and Skinner, concerned himself with individual human potential, originating from within the learner instead of conditioning that is controlled externally by the teacher.

The constructivist pedagogy originates from the psychological theories of Swiss developmental psychologist Jean-Paul Piaget, whose theory of cognitive development was based on his ideas of the learner's assimilation and accommodation of new knowledge. His ideas, which influenced the humanist school, extended beyond and into what is now understood as the constructivist framework for teaching. Piaget's understanding of pedagogy insisted that the student be an active participant in the learning process. His understanding of the individual's construction of mental models was that the process, though fueled by interactions with external experiences in the world, is mostly internal. Vygotsky took Piaget's learning theories to a whole new level when he introduced the role of language and sociocultural influences on the learning process. His understanding of how people use thought and language in their composition of new knowledge is complex and difficult to comprehend in relation to the simple elegance of the transfer model of learning. Vygotsky's idea about what happens when we learn is that we construct our own meaning of the world through our relationships with other people. Like Bandura, he believed that learning is social, and his understanding of the process is that it is also, as Bakhtin believed, personal and internal. Constructivists believe that we do not learn in a vacuum, apart from the influences of the past, our world, and culture. They do not think that that we acquire knowledge through passive and direct processes. They believe that we are constantly making and remaking our own novel understandings of the world through our daily experiences and social interactions. They believe that by combining new information we come by with that which we already know, we develop newer and newer theories about the way the world works, and that we are always unconsciously testing these new theories against our newest experiences as we encounter them.

The constructivist and humanist pedagogies are often grouped together as "liberal pedagogies" because they both place the development of individual human potential at the center of the learning process, focusing on experiential, social, and holistic educational experiences. Both the humanist and constructivist schools are concerned with human freedom, growth, and our potential for individual, optimal human performance instead of the coverage of knowledge sets and generalized skills-based curriculum.

Today's scientific pedagogies (standards-based, outcomes-based, and assessment-centered) can sometimes be designed to include more student-centered activity than in the past, but at their core, they are neither student-centered nor teacher-centered exclusively. Because scientific pedagogues value the acquisition of established canonical knowledge, they have put testing at the center of the learning process, edging out teachers and rolling over students. Liberal pedagogues value the spontaneity of our experience as a catalyzing force in our learning processes. Economist and philosopher Friedrich Hayek (1980) conceptualized the generation of new knowledge as a spontaneous occurrence, and he placed "learning" itself at the center of instructional interaction as opposed to placing the teacher, the student, a test, the culture, or a taxonomy of externally defined standards at the center of its pedagogy.

The classroom teacher whose pedagogy focuses on the spontaneous emergence of intellectual order is a liberal pedagogue using a multi-centric diffusion of instructional and curricular methodologies. Those who ascribe to the liberal approach hold that freely associated conversation, disequilibration, reflection, and the de-stigmatization of failure, as well as the explicit modeling of continuous inquiry and the regular questioning of otherwise culturally accepted knowledge claims or truths, laws, or facts are essential for students and teachers and ought not be mitigated by preordained goals, objectives, or idealized outcomes.

Liberal pedagogies are equally personal and impersonal. The tradition of the liberal approach extends back to Socrates and Confucius, Locke, Rousseau, and Kant, as well as Americans Thomas Jefferson and Ralph Waldo Emerson. Parker Palmer, a noted author and proponent of liberal education, exposes a semi-democratic/Quaker-esque community approach to teaching, understanding that the knowledge of truth has both an inner dimension as well as an interpersonal one and that learning is a journey of discovery through a personal past, a focus on the present, and focused attention to the future.

Vocational pedagogy is oriented toward the pragmatic training of specific technical skills through modeling, demonstration, and other experiential methods. Vocational education often pairs experts (teachers) with novices (students), who, through dialogue, experiential practice, failure, reflection, and other experiences, generate new understandings of specific technical procedures together as mentors and proteges navigating the field of technical knowledge and skill. American education philosopher and thinker John Dewey is well known as one of the most emphatic proponents of learning by doing, hands-on instruction, or experiential education. Dewey (1916) believed that technical knowledge comes from our experiences with the objects we encounter in life, especially while working. He said that it is "impossible to procure knowledge without the use of objects which impress the mind." In vocational education today, there is an emphasis on teaching practical, technical skills oriented toward specific careers. However, the idea of "career" has always been a socially constructed concept, and that concept is being radically reconstructed today. This trend of reconstructing the concept of a career will only accelerate in the years to come, causing a pressing need for reconceptualizing the definition of vocational education.

In 1916, Dewey warned that grounding vocational education too deeply in the practical application of technical skills in the pursuit of monetary rewards at the expense of understanding the meaning that one may extract from a vocation would erode the very concept of vocationalism. In fact, vocationalism is and always has been about having a specific creative purpose for one's work and the talents, skills, and mastery needed to fulfill that specific purpose by performing the work. Dewey equated vocational activity with art. Monetary rewards, hyper-utilitarianism, and external validation are, after all, only externally affirming and extrinsically fulfilling, and they cannot and are not enough to sustain vocationalism today. Even as policymakers have made recent and desperate attempts to reinvest in vocational education, they continue to miss how necessary intrinsic and intellectual validation is in vocational education because policymakers have since Dewey's time framed vocational education in a dualistic paradigm where vocational education is more closely associated with technical training than liberal education.

That mistake aside, vocational education is not the same thing as vocational pedagogy and never has been. Vocational pedagogy is a pure concept where the teacher is a mentor and the student is an apprentice. Vocational pedagogy is the father of experiential education. It is distinct from liberal, traditional, and scientific pedagogies because vocation is the exercise of intelligence within an activity, not apart from it. Vocationalism is framed by craftsmanship, and vocational pedagogy is not exclusive to technical training. It is methodologically useful as a means of teaching and learning in many fields, professions, and intellectual paradigms, not just in the teaching of trades. The best example of vocational pedagogy might be medical school.

Critical pedagogy was originated by Brazilian educator and philosopher Paolo Freire, who rejected the idea that knowledge can be politically neutral and that access to and the exchange of knowledge are restricted by those in power to maintain that power. Freire argued that whether teachers are aware of the politics inherent in their teaching or not, the dynamic of their instruction is informed by and perpetuates a distinct power dynamic, sometimes one that even robs them of their own power. He believed that traditional Western methods of instruction reinforce many forms of societal oppression (political, economic, spiritual, psychological, and others) by conditioning people at the earliest age (before they are developmentally able to enter into inquiry) to exchange their freedom for assimilation. Critical pedagogy seeks to expose the insidiousness of colonial thinking in teaching and the auto-domestication of teachers and students.

Although like liberal pedagogies in many ways, *the goal of critical pedagogy is emancipation from oppression through our awareness of how power dynamics are embedded in our curriculum, teaching philosophy, and culture*. Critical theorists hold that true liberation can only come from education systems devoid of oppression. Critical pedagogy is an especially philosophic set of ideas combined through intersectionality with the practical application of theory through political, artistic, and intellectual means. A main concentration of its energy is on examining how the structure of social classism manifests in both dominant intellectual and popular cultures, perpetrated through traditional education institutions via conditioning and through repeating traditional socioeconomic narratives and calling them curricula. Critical pedagogy is constantly extending anew into the political, cultural, and academic consciousness. Henry Giroux, a professor of history and English at McMaster University, and Peter McLaren, a professor of critical studies at Chapman University, have since the 1980s represented, redefined, and applied the ideas of critical pedagogy in their teaching and writing, exposing authoritarian tendencies in American education systems and cultures that connect knowledge with power.

Other leading academics who have represented the ideas of critical pedagogy and have been associated with critical pedagogy are bell hooks, Joe Kincholoe, Howard Zinn, Michael Apple, Johnathan Kozol, John Holt, and Parker Palmer. Whereas other pedagogies do not take political stands, critical pedagogues are aggressively anti-racist, ardently feminist, staunchly pro-queer, and openly post-colonial. Theirs is a theory of discourse, engaging in the purposeful disruption of traditional power structures that are embedded in the American education tradition. This pedagogy is characterized by an epistemological cynicism that decenters structuralist notions of teaching while promoting pure freedom and democracy. In application, theirs is a practice centered on inquiry, problem-posing, and antagonistic discourse. Like liberal pedagogues, critical pedagogues not only value the freedom of the individual but also champion it. However, their execution of educational activity and practice has freedom as an end, as an objective, and as an outcome, and therefore does not center the learning process on knowledge, skills, or growth in and of itself.

Why Pedagogy Matters

The threshold between curriculum and pedagogy has been historically vague. And the persistent idea that pedagogy is about teaching methods and strategies as if they are the same as various approaches to instruction also confounds anyone trying to conceptualize the basic essence of the term. Ultimately, this strange word refers to the academic examination of processes used in the acquisition or assimilation of new knowledge by an individual in an educational context. This epistemology considers the various types of interactions that take place during learning. Those interactions are governed by our beliefs about how people learn. They become instructional methodologies, teaching practices, and the substance of our curriculum.

Pedagogy is not the same as instruction or curriculum. It is more than style or approach. It lies just deeply enough underneath these to govern our decisions without our full appreciation of its power. I'm glad she asked me what pedagogy is, because, as much as I know about education, I have a lot to learn, and like so many of my students over the years, she is teaching me with her curiosity. As I consider what this word means to me, "personally," as I consider what "my own pedagogy" might be, I ask myself questions like: Why am I drawn to teaching as my life's work? What do I think teaching is? How do people learn? What is more important: the what (curriculum), the how (instruction), or the why (pedagogy)? And what is most important? The students' well-being, their intellectual growth? Their readiness to enter adulthood?

Repeatedly, I am drawn to the image of an ancient Greek servant walking children to school. I imagine walking along a dirt road in Athens or Sparta, serving as a humble master, a calm and composed guide, protecting my precious and vulnerable charges. Do I crave simplicity? Teaching is a complex and sophisticated profession that is forever expanding. Exhausting and even overwhelming, I find it impossible to do the job adequately. Am I yearning for a role that, though not necessarily easier, might be less all-consuming? Is it the simplicity of "guiding as teaching" that attracts me? I have, over the course of my career, moved away from *telling and showing* to teaching, gravitating toward the role of a Sherpa, who helps climbers up the mountain but doesn't show them how to climb it or tell them how beautiful the view is. I have become less hands-on as a teacher and more present and conscious of the example I might set for my students.

A Final Thought

When I was a young child in school, I was a sensitive boy who was often frightened of the teachers and the other students. Sadly, my vulnerability was easy for the bullies to see. Ultimately, it's not the ideas, thoughts, and facts of the image of a servant who walks children to school that are appealing to me, it's more the feelings that imagining that scene evokes. Although it's too late to protect a much younger me from the abuse from his peers and the neglect of his teachers, it's not too late to watch over, and be the quiet guardian of children (and adults), protecting them from their peers, their teachers, and even from themselves.

· 7 ·

THE GRAVITY OF BEING

"For me, teaching is about love. It is not about transferring information but rather creating an atmosphere of mystery and imagination and discovery. When I begin to lose myself because of some unresolved pain or fears or the overpowering feelings of shame, then I no longer teach. I deliver information, and I think I become irrelevant then."

Brené Brown, Daring Greatly

If we agree that teaching only occurs when someone is learning, then trust is vital for teaching because learning is essentially about changing. Whether learners change themselves by assimilating new information into their knowledge base, new skill sets into their mental toolbox, or replacing old beliefs with new ones, learning is fundamentally about the transformation from one state to another. Those changes may be physical, psychological, emotional, spiritual, or, simultaneously, any combination of all of these. People will generally resist anyone helping them change unless they trust that person. My main interest as a schoolteacher has been the cognitive growth (change) of my students, though my definition has been expanding to other areas of growth over the years. Growth is change. Development is change, and these changes are inevitable, and our role in them is not guaranteed. The teacher's role, intentional or not, is conditional. Our students must let us in. And that does not happen without some level of trust. The more trust there is, the more potential there is for learning. Trust requires vulnerability, not force; freedom, not control; heart, not mind; and understanding rather than judgment and courage in the face of fear.

Any teacher who does not have strong relationships with their students and whose students do not trust them for whatever reason may think they are teaching and that their students are learning, but they are not. Sometimes, as teachers, we violate their trust. We are all fallible and capable of making mistakes. This requires healing, repair, and making amends before a new trust can be established. However, if we never build trust in the first place, then there is no relationship, or if we build a fragile trust, the relationship is weak. When we make our relationships with students conditional on their compliance, those relationships are transactional instead of collaborative, and they fail. Real teaching requires authentic interaction, needs a relational exchange of heart and mind, and only rises to the level of real learning when it comes from the heart as much as the head. This is why compliance-based or transactional student-teacher relationships are limited in their ability to transcend knowing to a place of understanding.

The force that compliance-based teaching calls for reduces, even negates, trust. The more force we employ in our teaching, the less freedom our students have. Adolescents need freedom. Any reduction of freedom erodes the very trust that is essential for students to open up to us, to set aside their egos, to accept that they do not already know everything about the world, and to be vulnerable in front of us and their classmates. They need us to model for them how to be vulnerable, which means we must be brave and be first to expose our flanks, to be our imperfect selves with them, to admit we are wrong sometimes, and to admit that we are not always right, not all knowing, and not invincible. This is the very last thing we want to do with groups of adolescents all day long, but it is what is required. If we live in fear, they live in fear, and then deep learning is not at all possible. The biggest problem with fear is that it naturally leads to force, and force is not compatible with learning. In turn, force leads back to more fear. Without confronting what we fear about ourselves and the world, we become controlling and manipulative. We nudge, coerce, and even push our students. And, without even realizing it, we make them the means to our ends. Worse, we make them the means to other people's ends, people who don't even know our students.

Whenever we are growing, as a fetus in the womb, a child at home with our family, or as an adolescent venturing out into the world, we are unprotected. Think of the caterpillar in its cocoon. Now, think of that fuzzy little worm without the case to keep it warm, disguised, and safe from predators. Nearly every adolescent will, relative to their dependence on post-pubescent years, eventually become a powerful adult who is able to ignore the various daily attacks the world launches or counter those attacks in various ways, ultimately preserving their sense of self. Teachers naturally see the butterfly.

We know that everything is going to be okay. But the caterpillar doesn't know that. Adolescents have never experienced growing up before. These are two critical truths. Theirs and ours. These truths co-exist alongside one another in our classrooms every day. One truth, ours, says that the adolescent will be okay. The other one says that they might not be. This is a *sacred dialogic tension*, demanding our most *resolute awareness*. Their cocoons hang before us in the immediacy of the present moment. We won't see it if we are not present. The less present we are for their transformation, the less likely they will be to open their eyes to it, even though the "it" in this case is their very own metamorphosis from a slug hanging encased in a gray paper sleeping bag to a beautiful, winged creature soaring with the wind.

Adolescents, some more so than others, doubt that they will ever possess those wings that are so clearly protruding from our backs—the backs of their parents—the ones that they see on most adults. Who can blame them? Adolescence is fraught with assaults on identity, ego, and self-efficacy. These are the very same wings we forget we have. We take our powers, our independence, and our abilities to sustain ourselves for granted, and we do it every day. When we know that they will fly, we are right. They will. However, they are right too. Change is dangerous. This is a crucial and very sensitive time for their psyches, for their identities, and for their self-efficacy. The *sacred dialogic tension*. Think of how often you forget that you have the powers you possess, "your wings." Imagine that your wings are either very small, have not even broken through the skin yet, or are there but have never been tried out. Now, think of your students. That's how they feel.

This is what my mentor, Bob Cunningham, calls "the gravity of being." He taught me that adolescents are drawn to "the immediacy of the moment, because that is the only place where freedom exists." Given that there is a trusting relationship initiated by our own vulnerability, this gravity creates an authentic and shared understanding of reality in that present moment, arising out of *communitas*. Transient, personal, and experienced together with our students, in a state where we are at least temporarily and perhaps hypothetically on the same level, this is an infinitely more powerful state than any that can be achieved through the mere application of force. In fact, this state is impossible to arrive at through the use of force. In the present moment, with trust, community, and the relative safety of identity and emotion, we and our students can be drawn toward and accomplish nearly any objective, even if the goal is as difficult or as easy as changing one's mind. In this state, we possess a unified, shared understanding of the idea of what a class is. We are a group of "students" gathered to learn something together. This community is more powerful than any stated instructional objective or teaching method. Community is transcendence.

Another Mistake

I say, moreover, that you make a great, a very great mistake if you think that psychology, being the science of the mind's laws, is something from which you can deduce definite programs and schemes and methods of instruction for immediate schoolroom use. Psychology is a science, and teaching is an art; and sciences never generate arts directly out of themselves.

William James, *Talks to Teachers on Psychology and to Students on Some of Life's Ideals*

There are few more noteworthy curriculum theorists in the 20th century than Ralph Tyler, whose model of objectives-based education has become the centerpiece of American education today. Yet, the objectives given by the teacher are not necessarily "understood in concert" with the students. Ralph Tyler was an American educator who pioneered education assessment. His principles deeply influenced the underlying policies of education systems in the United States and around the world from the mid-20th century to the present day. The Elementary and Secondary Education Act of 1965, based on his thinking, made outcome-based curricula law. His book, *Basic Principles of Curriculum and Instruction* (1949), made curriculum pre-eminent in schooling. It defined the concept of curriculum in such a way that other education thinkers based their work on his description. For example, the *backward design* idea of Grant Wiggins and Jay McTighe (2005) would not exist without Tyler's *Basic Principles*, published nearly 50 years earlier. It made the "what" more important than the "how" or the "why" or the "who." And this concept of curriculum is based solely on objectifiable, measurable phenomena.

Tyler based his conceptual framework on one seemingly logical question for schools, assuming that the adults who run them ought to control teaching and learning. And all at once, Tyler's legacy was cemented into parallel beliefs that still hold today. The first is that teaching is a science that can be engineered for both teachers and students through competent curriculum development. And the second is that learning objectives must originate from external sources—from outside the student, from outside the teacher, and even from outside the school. The question is: What educational purposes should schools seek to attain for students? Most people who know about Tyler, think of him as the father of curriculum, but at heart, he was trained as and acted as *an evaluator*, which is why measuring outcomes was extremely important to him. Tyler's approach was scientific. His assumptions about teaching were based on linear thinking, and his teaching experience was just about as minimal as experience can be.

After only one year teaching high school science, Tyler began to ask how teachers can design learning experiences that are likely to be useful in attaining the purposes of academic learning. He wanted to know how schools can get students to do what we want them to do, change the way we want them to change, and know what we want them to know. If that sounds forceful, it is. It is the basis of the modern compliance model of education.

Then he asked, How can those defined learning experiences be organized for effective instruction? So, not only the "what" (curriculum) must be controlled by school leaders, but the methods or "how" (instructions) used to teach that curriculum must also be controlled by school leaders. There is not a lot of autonomy here, is there? Not for teachers or students. Tyler's one year of experience teaching high school science led him to the erroneous conclusion that both teachers and students must be controlled by external forces; otherwise, learning will not take place.

Tyler also wanted to know: how can the learning experiences that we select be evaluated? Of course, this evaluation is used to make judgments to facilitate a data-driven process of revising the methods that were deemed ineffective at controlling the outcome. Although Tyler's book (1949) describes a model of learning that is situated through the action of the student, it is "the student" that seems to be reduced to an object in this paradigm. On page 63 of *Basic Principles of Curriculum and Instruction*, Tyler writes of the student's role: "It is what he does that he learns, not what the teacher does," but what Tyler does is ignores the fact that students are human beings, and adolescents in particular have ideas and interests of their own. They desire autonomy just like we do, even if they are not always ready to be completely responsible for themselves. They do not come to school as blank slates. They have their own memories and life histories, have lived their own experiences, possess their own ideas about themselves and life, and have constructed their own theories about the world. They have their own fears, wounds, and dreams.

Compliance is about force, and outcome-based education requires a rigorous compliance system for it to have any effect. Whether we call this system a standards-based system, an objectives-based system, or an outcomes-based system, ultimately they are all based on one simple prerequisite. That prerequisite is the system's need to control, through agency, every child's thinking and behavior as much as possible to accomplish those outcomes that are externally imposed on the child.

This schema of schooling places the teacher as an agent of the system, using psychological controls like conditioning systems with rewards and punishments that work well on mice, dogs, and ducks but are less effective for humans and impede the basic processes of higher levels of learning. The other fact is that outcome-based education, though sometimes useful for adult technical, medical, and legal training, usually has more negative side effects than could possibly ever be balanced out by the positive ones. Chief among those are the employment of force and fear to accomplish the compliance necessary to move children in a learning process that many adolescents naturally resist for a myriad of reasons.

The fusion of scientific behavioral psychology and its theories of conditioning combined with micro-economic mindsets has led to an objectification of the K-12 education model that leaves no room for the humanity of individual students. Because, like Tyler, most policymakers have little classroom experience, they do not see the flaw in thinking about education as both a system of control and a means of control. They only see it as a means to their objective ends. To them, teaching is a science, requiring strict formulas and defined processes. This is the ultimate mistake in education. Teaching is not a science.

Back in 1899, while at Harvard, William James gave his historic public lectures on psychology to the school teachers of Cambridge, Massachusetts. Since then, these lectures have been published and reprinted many times as *Talks to Teachers on Psychology and to Students on Some of Life's Ideals*. He warned us 124 years ago that applying the tenets of behavioral science in their purest form to teaching is neither practical nor prudent. James said:

> To know psychology, therefore, is absolutely no guarantee that we shall be good teachers. To advance to that result, we must have an additional endowment altogether, a happy tact and ingenuity to tell us what definite things to say and do when the pupil is before us. That ingenuity in meeting and pursuing the pupil, that tact for the concrete situation, though they are the alpha and omega of the teacher's art, are things to which psychology cannot help us in the least.

James warned us then, and it would serve us well to finally recognize now that teaching cannot be reduced to any scientific method. He regarded "divination and perception" as more powerful tools for teachers than conditioning and control, but James was as mystified by what teachers do as Tyler and Thorndike were apt to trivialize teaching. What none of them understand is that what we do requires skills that extend far beyond what science can provide. We engage logic and intuition; reason and imagination; head and heart; technical skill and creativity; interpersonal and intrapersonal intellect; extrinsic and intrinsic motivation; and most importantly, we use science—but mostly as part of an ever imperfect, always incomplete, and wholly complex artistic pursuit of knowledge with our students.

James warned the Cambridge teachers that making teaching a science means reducing it to tactics:

> The science of psychology, and whatever science of general pedagogics may be based on it, are in fact much like the science of war. Nothing is simpler or more definite than the principles of either. In war, all you have to do is to work your enemy into a position from which the natural obstacles prevent him from escaping if he tries to; then to fall on him in numbers superior to his own, at a moment when you have led him to think you far away; and so, with a minimum of exposure of your own troops, to hack his force to pieces, and take the remainder prisoners. Just so, in teaching, you must simply work your pupil into such a state of interest in what you are going to teach him that every other object of attention is banished from his mind; then reveal it to him so impressively that he will remember the occasion to his dying day; and finally fill him with devouring curiosity to know what the next steps in connection with the subject are....

That's all. As my father used to say, "A piece of cake." Right? Although we might set James's sarcasm aside, we must honor his overall cynicism. Unfortunately, it seems that either we have learned nothing from James or that we understand him perfectly and dismiss his sage advice because of our lack of imagination to move past an overly simplistic, empirically formulaic mode of thinking with regards to teaching and learning.

Fear is historically rudimentary to teaching, and this is a fact left sitting in plain sight but one we don't ever discuss. Ironically, we are too afraid to. This is unfortunate because it is unnecessary. As a result, this fear, embedded in students and teachers alike, festers. And it grows. It hardens us. We use it to intimidate our students, our colleagues, and our bosses. And our students, bosses, and colleagues do the same to us and for the same reason. Fear. We compete instead of collaborating. We argue instead of sharing. We defend our positions because we are so afraid of being wrong. If our lives depend on being right, is this the war James refers to or an amygdala hijacking? We even lie to our students and ourselves to cover up our mistakes, our errors, and our failures, consequently teaching them to hide their mistakes. Showing them that they need to hide the very natural misconceptions, errors, and mistakes that are an essential part of the learning process. This situation cripples both students and teachers. As teachers, we must have access to our students' failures, their misconceptions, and their errors. We cannot teach them, and they cannot learn, if we do not know what they do not know. But why should they trust us with their failures when we shame them? Why should they trust us if we don't trust them? How can we expect them to be vulnerable while we have our academic armor on? How can we teach our students how to revise their thinking if we don't show that we are constantly revising ours? Learning. And even if their thoughts are poorly hidden, we still can't go near them because a student who hides their ideas is not ready to acknowledge that those very ideas may have been misconceived, not yet. They hide their ideas because they see us hiding ours.

More often than we realize, they do what we do. Modeling is perhaps such a powerful factor in the dynamic between the teacher and student, more powerful than any explicitly direct instruction, that we traffic our fear of change, insidiously spreading fear and fundamentally encouraging it at the same time. We ultimately teach with and to fear, using it as a means of control and toward our ends or the ones we represent, as the fear eats away at our potential like a parasite nibbling through an enormous cocoon where the butterfly of teaching and learning is encased.

Force and teaching are not congruent. Maslow showed us that force is a hammer devoid of heart, the utter absence of Noddings' "ethic of care" that must be central to our efforts in helping children grow. Again, to quote James:

> ...The principles being so plain, there would be nothing but victories for the masters of the science, either on the battlefield or in the schoolroom, if they did not both have to make their application to an incalculable quantity in the shape of the mind of their opponent. The mind of your own enemy, the pupil, is working away from you as keenly and eagerly as is the mind of the commander on the other side from the scientific general. Just what the respective enemies want and think, and what they know and do not know, are as hard things for the teacher as for the general to find out. Divination and perception, not psychological pedagogics or theoretic strategy, are the only helpers here.

A Final Thought

Our tradition of schooling is so grounded in a culture of fear and force that it takes a conscious effort and a brave heart to confront fear in our teaching. It took me years before I had the courage to abandon what I assumed my role as a teacher was, years to let go of the paradigm of the student-teacher relationship I was trained to apply in my work, years to stop listening to my department chair and colleagues, to ignore their advice and even their direction.

I had to fail over and over again at teaching before I was forced to see that I couldn't make it work. I hated being forced to do things when I was a kid, and I hate it now. I even hate being forced to do things that I typically enjoy. If you forced me to go fly fishing with you, to listen to my favorite music with you, to eat a gourmet Italian meal, and then to take a nap, I would resent it and resent you. And then I would no longer love those things as I do now. So, if you forced me to do something I did not understand or something I already thought I did not like, I would do more than resent it. I would resist it, and I would resist you. After failing for a year trying to manipulate, entice, coerce, and force my students to learn, I had an epiphany. And this is what it was.

I can't do it that way. There is a long-standing tradition of using teacher authority to force students to learn. I hate being forced to do things. And I knew, even back then, that my students did too. I didn't need them to like me, but I wanted to avoid making them hate me because that made teaching harder than it had to be. It made building trusting relationships with them very difficult.

So, one day, I did a little experiment. I gave my students a little freedom that I normally would not have. And I had proof that I was right about my guess almost immediately. They responded positively. They appreciated even a tiny bit of trust, freedom, and faith in them. Our relationship turned on that moment. I was being real with them—authentic and not forceful. I was not lying, I was not pushing them, and I was not trying to make them learn. I was letting it happen while at the same time being me. I was accepting that things might not go the way I planned. It was a powerful shift, and I never looked back.

My desperation drove me to stop pushing myself to teach and stop pushing them to learn. Without the manipulation, the coercion, and the sheer force of consequences, backed by a system of adult authority, a space opened up for us. In his book, *The Courage to Teach*, Parker Palmer says:

> ... to teach is to create a space in which the community of truth is practiced... I need to spend less time filling the space with data and my own thoughts and more time opening a space where students can have a conversation with the subject and with each other... (p.123)

When I reflect on Palmer's words, I understand what he was talking about. I know that relationships occupy a "space" in our lives. Palmer's abstract theory of a learning "space" is not possible when fear is present. And force breeds fear in our students through our denial of their autonomy. John Dewey described school in this way when he wrote his "Pedagogic Creed" in 1897 for *School Journal*. He wrote:

> I believe that the school is primarily a social institution. Education being a social process, the school is simply that form of community life in which all those agencies are concentrated that will be most effective in bringing the child to share in the inherited resources of the race, and to use his own powers for social ends... The teacher is not in the school to impose certain ideas or to form certain habits in the child, but is there as a member of the community to select the influences which shall affect the child and to assist him in properly responding to these. Thus the teacher becomes a partner in the learning process, guiding students to independently discover meaning within the subject area.

· 8 ·

MINDFULNESS

> Mindfulness is a state of mind that results from drawing novel distinctions, examining information from new perspectives, and being sensitive to context. It is an open, creative, probabilistic state of mind in which the individual might be led to finding differences among things thought similar and similarities among things thought different.
>
> E.J. Langer(1993; pp. 43–50).

Mindfulness is the practice of attending to the present moment. It is developed through meditation or other methods and is extremely useful for teaching and learning. Derived from Buddhist and Hindu traditions, it is a mental phenomenon where focusing on past experiences, present situations, and future plans is released to enter a *state of being* that centers the individual physically, spiritually, emotionally, and mentally in the present.

Psychological researchers have been exploring the state of *mindfulness* and its therapeutic value for the past few decades, developing some effective therapeutic applications based on *mindfulness*. These therapies have helped people who suffer from psychological conditions such as depression, anxiety, phobias, post-traumatic stress disorder (PTSD), addiction, and attention deficit hyperactivity disorder (ADHD).

After the publication of the book *The Power of Mindful Learning* in 2016 by Harvard psychologist and *mindfulness* researcher Ellen Langer, the concept of using *mindfulness* as a practice in K-12 schools has become more common. In fact, the application of *mindfulness* in schools has been a growing and important part of SEL curricula, with the goal of helping students and teachers build empathy for others, reduce anxiety, and decrease stress in the classroom. Based on broad meta-analyses, scholars argue that the application of *mindfulness* practices enhances the goals of education in the 21st century, which include adapting to rapid societal changes and fostering an ethic of care for other people. The use of *mindfulness* practices in K-12 schools has helped improve students' attention, focus, emotional regulation, and creativity. According to one large-scale German study conducted in 2014, students' problem-solving skills are also enhanced by using mindfulness practices in the classroom. Studies (Eklund et al., 2017) have found that mindfulness is linked to a variety of social, emotional, cognitive, and behavioral factors for adolescents and that it can be used to "prevent school expulsion" and academic failure. It also has the potential to improve students' social, emotional, behavioral, and cognitive control—all necessary traits for improving student achievement and academic outcomes. Langer (2016) writes that:

> Virtually all of our facts depend on context. For example, one plus one does not equal two in all number systems. More graphically, one wad of chewing gum plus one wad of chewing gum equals one wad of gum, not two. If we learn mindfully, we are more likely to realize this.

It starts with us

If we model mindful behavior, our students are likely to become more mindful. It's great to talk to students about *mindfulness* and to explicitly teach practices for *mindfulness*, but if we are not mindful ourselves, teaching *mindfulness* will not work. They tend to do what we do.

So, how can a typical schoolteacher become a more mindful person?

1. Start by not taking your smartphone to bed with you, and when you wake up in the morning, don't check your email or look for text messages while in bed. Instead, take 60 seconds to: *listen for sounds* (maybe there are birds outside the window), *move* and *sense* your toes or fingers, *feel* your breath, and *feel* the air moving in and out through your nose, filling your chest, and out through your mouth. Because *mindfulness* is a practice and requires practice, cultivating mindfulness is not merely about what you do when you are in the classroom. It is a way of being.

2. Then, *take notice* of your surroundings—your room, the walls, and the ceiling—without judgment, without thinking, and without planning anything.
3. You can check your email or Twitter literally after you have climbed out of bed. Wait until after a shower and a cup of coffee if you can, all the while *remaining curious*, observant, and meditatively aware of your surroundings.
4. When you arrive at your parking space, the school door, or your classroom door, *try to notice something new* that you have never seen before. Look for what is out of place. Notice something that has always been there but that you have never looked at completely.
5. Seconds before any of your classes begin, before your students arrive, *stand in the doorway to your classroom* or entrance to your learning environment. Take a breath or two, and without thinking about all the things you must do (10 seconds tops), smile to yourself.
6. When students begin to arrive for class, *greet each one by name at the door*, smiling if you can, and think to yourself as each one passes: How is Jorgé? How is Amelia? How is Emma? How is Matt? Try to sense what each student is feeling, experiencing, or thinking as they pass. You won't be able to, but try. The point is not to *know*. It is to instead *notice*. This may lead you to observe something that you otherwise may have missed: a student who is sad, lost, or disconnected. You may sense conflict, chaos, and harmony; let's hope. Although teachers already have enough to do, we do not need to plug in another extension to the endless list of cables that are plugged into and draw current from our finite cognitive load. This work is not only integral to teaching; it saves more energy than it takes. You will miss a few who get past you. Maybe one student will ask you something, and you won't see another student walk by. Listen to the student with the question. Consider carefully what they are asking and what they need. Answer if you can. It's okay that you don't see all of them as they walk past. You are not taking attendance. You are being present for your students. And modeling a way for them to be. You must do this nearly every day, for every class, for it to work.
7. This is about *you*, not your students. As much as you are taking a moment to see your students, you are doing it primarily to enhance your own well-being and your own calmness. Some of them will likely feel seen. There will be consequences for that—not as subtle as you

may expect, either. All of them are good—some immediately, others, eventually. They might see you too, and they may reap the benefits of mindfulness, as well. They may be calmer, more centered, more focused, more open, less stressed, less aggressive, more observant, and more ready to learn. It's for you, not them. They might learn from your daily example about how to be in the world, about how to be more mindful, how to pay attention, how to be more patient, and how to notice others. But! Do it for you, primarily. Do it for yourself, because we ought to take care of ourselves. Maybe our students will learn from our example to take care of their selves, too.

How do I Teach My Students to be Mindful?

We don't have to tell them we are teaching them about mindfulness. We don't even have to tell them what exactly we are doing or why we are doing it if we think that will be a distraction, but when we teach our students to be mindful, they will be more effective learners. First, we do this by being mindful of ourselves. Then, if we create mindful activities for them that they will do during the class period, day, or year, they can learn to be curious, ask questions, ask for help, focus on what is important, cooperate, make better decisions, and self-regulate—all necessary characteristics of good learners. Some will be part of the curriculum, others won't. Here are some ideas.

1. *Begin class with a one-minute mindful activity.* This could be a minute of guided meditation, an ungraded and uncollected freewrite, a story about your dog, the reading of a short poem, listening to a song, a "stand and stretch," or making up your own mindfulness activity. It should not be required or count toward a grade. I repeat. It should not be mandatory. The only thing they have to do is remain silent for one minute. The first time you do this, they might not be completely silent, but be patient; after a few days, they will gradually look forward to it. As will you.
2. *When you see a student who is being mindful, acknowledge it subtly.* This is not meant to be a reward or positive reinforcement. It may be, and that's fine, but it is meant to be a reciprocation of mindfulness. You are being mindful of that student's mindful behavior. Mindfulness leads to more mindfulness. Noticing might mean you gently tap your finger on a student's desk, and when she looks up, you smile, making eye contact.

3. During class or during the day, *listen actively* to your students when they talk to you, making eye contact, letting them finish their thought or question, and asking them questions about what they are talking about.
4. *Focus more on the processes* of learning than the outcomes. If a student writes a good sentence or paragraph, instead of praising him or her, ask what his or her process was, what steps he or she took to write it, and how he or she came up with the words in a particular order. Make it clear that the writing is very good, but emphasize the student's method, not the product. You could do this privately (in a conference) or publicly (during a class discussion), depending on the student and the situation. Ask, "How exactly did you construct this sentence? It is very good."
5. *Take an art break.* This could be scheduled into a lesson plan or available at all times, depending on your style of teaching and the needs of the moment. This requires having some simple art supplies available in the corner of the classroom or in a closet. Markers, paper, paint, colored pencils, poster board, glue, beads, string, cardboard, and clay are ok if you have the funds, but it's just as good, if not better, to use junk for art supplies. Ask your students to bring broken shells from the beach, old magazines, sticks, leaves, sand, rocks, and cut-up cardboard boxes. You buy the glue. Use recycled milk containers for storage, and give a different student each week extra credit for having the job of keeping the art corner well stocked and clean.

Other Ideas for Creating Mindful Activities

Mindful walking: Teach your students how to pay attention to their footsteps as they walk.

Field trips to the state park or the beach: Take your students on a free field trip to a local place where they can freewrite, discuss a book, or explore the natural world.

Singing a song: Make a song that relates to a lesson or topic, or sing one that someone has already made up.

Creative writing: Allow your students to write poems or stories about the subject you are trying to teach them about. Don't grade them! If you must give them credit, tell them it's a pass or fail assignment, and give everyone *pass*, never fail.

Poetry readings: Have monthly poetry readings where students voluntarily choose poems (that you preview and approve) they want to read aloud to the class for extra credit. This can be done in math class too.

Stand up, take a breath and sit down: Pretty self-explanatory.

Storytime: On Mondays, start each class by telling a five minute story from your weekend that may have a hidden lesson in it related to the week's curriculum. Students can contribute stories too, once they have heard a few of yours.

Mindful eating: Teach students how to eat a piece of fruit, a cookie or even chips in a mindful way. Buddhist monk and peace activist, Thich Nhat Hanh, has written about this. I'm sure it won't take long to find his meditation on eating a tangerine with a quick Google search.

Celebrate failure: To encourage students to admit they are confused, and to stay with that confusion until they have gained understanding, create a practice of celebrating failure, misunderstanding and mistakes that teach lessons. Start by celebrating your own failure.

Share dreams: These could be dreams you have had in your sleep or goals. This could be done on a class blog.

Googleculturalinstitute: This website allows children to discover artistic collections from around the world without leaving the classroom. Explore cultural treasures and use these as inspiration for centering a class in the moment.

Sit on the floor: Do this on a Friday afternoon for 10 minutes. This will help you and your students to be more grounded. If students don't want to do this, don't make them.

Get rid of desks: Traditional classroom furniture was designed to create barriers between teachers and students. Eliminate these barriers if you can.

Google 20% time: Take one day out of each week to allow students to explore subjects (loosely situated within an academic area) that they are interested in. Also known as "side project time," Google's 20% started a practice where company employees were given 20% of their paid time to pursue personal projects that were related to Google's mission. The objective of the program is to inspire innovation. Google's 20% Project was not the first time this level of employee autonomy was incorporated into a company practice. In 1948, the manufacturing company 3M allowed its employees to use 15% of their paid work time to pursue personal interests. This practice was made famous when a 3M employee named Arthur Fry invented the Post-It note during his 15% time. Google's commitment to this level of freedom for its employees paid off for them as well. Gmail was created during that time, and it is the most popular email service in the world.

Google Translate, Google Maps, Google Street View, Google Talk, Google News, and Google Sky were also created during that time.

Low tone time: Set aside a specific period of time where everyone talks in a low tone. This will increase their ability to listen overall.

Close your eyes: Occasionally, even randomly assign students to close their eyes for 30 seconds and listen to their breathing.

Celebrate differences: When there is a discovery that someone is unique, for example, if there is a new student in class who is blind or deaf, ask him or her if it would be okay if the class had a 15-minute Q&A about blindness. Many blind people don't mind talking about it at all. In fact, they prefer it over the whispers. Or, if a student has lived outside of the United States, ask them what that was like.

Five minute birthday parties: Ask students to write their birthdates on an index card and hand them in to you on the very first day of class (if they want to), and then celebrate birthdays as they come up with a single nut-free cupcake for that person, playing a recording of the Beatles' "birthday." You can find it on YouTube. A giant homemade card that everyone signs also works well. For those students whose birthdays fall on the weekend or summer, schedule an *alternative school year birthday* with them.

Sign the cast: If someone breaks their arm, make sure you allow time for the whole class to sign their cast or a card. Of course, you will ask that student if signing the cast is okay, first, and in private, before you move on from that.

Status of the class: Hold a weekly meeting (usually held for 30 minutes on a Friday afternoon) where students can make suggestions for how the class could be run better. Whenever, during *our class meetings*, a student voiced an idea that made sense, I would shower them with praise and then ask the class if they agreed. If there was consensus, I would ask the student who came up with it if they would like to be in charge of implementing the idea.

Mindlessness Vs. Mindfulness?

"The style of education that concentrates on outcomes generally also presents facts unconditionally. This approach encourages mindlessness. If something is accepted as accepted truth, alternative ways of thinking do not even come up for consideration."

Ellen Langer, *Mindfulness*

Langer's 30 years of research have revealed that mindlessness is expensive and that the benefits of mindfulness are significant across many aspects of our lives. Mindfulness leads directly to competence in almost every area, while also reducing the number and severity of accidents. It enhances and expands our ability to remember, to create, and to reduce stress. It improves health outcomes and expands longevity, and for our purposes, it empowers us to learn deeply and sustainably. Unfortunately, some of our most common messages to students in school run counter to what we know about mindfulness and how to effect powerful learning.

Instead of using mindfulness, we sometimes:

- *Encourage mindlessness.* We do this using two diametrically opposed yet habitual teaching methods. The first method has become a tradition in education, and that is the method of forcing repetition. When we teach students to repeat things over and over, they are conditioned to rely on a dangerous mindset. For example, think of how driving a familiar route in your car can often cause you to reach your destination without thinking. This is less than an ideal state of mind for learning at the conceptual level. We are unconscious, asleep at the wheel, and unaware of ourselves. This is not learning.
- The second mindlessness teaching method we have championed occurs when we are first exposed to new information. Often, when we are introduced to new information, *we process it without question.* In fact, questioning new information is sometimes discouraged in classrooms. Instead of entertaining inquiry and presenting alternative perspectives on the information, we encourage students to swallow it whole, ingesting it in mindless gulps. By processing new information in this mindless fashion, we commit to a singular understanding of it.
- Though unintentional, *we foster mindlessness by presenting facts as closed cases*, ignoring other possible perspectives. Scientists understand that when their research findings seem "true," they are only valid within the context of the experiment or the conditions of the study. However, education research often phrases such possibilities—not as probabilities but instead as absolute statements of objective fact—dismissing the actual uncertainty of not merely that circumstance but of any given "reality."

Encouraged by high-stakes testing, teachers often do the same. This is unfortunate, given how much more interesting and curious statements of probability are than statements of certainty. Presenting the facts of the world as solved equations, as objective reality, or as the truth can only lead our students to close their minds without wondering if and when such information may or may not be true. This cuts off their opportunity to be curious about how changing one fact to its opposite can turn a complete system on its head. According to Langer (2016), facts are not free of context. What they mean and how they are useful are dependent on the given situation in which they are embedded. Therefore, it is important to acknowledge that facts are not divorced from perception or interpretation.

A Final Thought

Building a mindful environment in our classrooms gives your students a space where they know they are safe and their thoughts and feelings are respected. It may take some students longer to participate in mindful activities because they have not experienced them before. But that's okay. We cannot and should not force students to be mindful, and that is the point. By including mindfulness practices as a regular part of our classroom culture, we are showing our students we are mindful of them and allowing the space for them to do the same.

· 9 ·

FORCE AND TRAUMA

> Traumatized people chronically feel unsafe inside their bodies: The past is alive in the form of gnawing interior discomfort. Their bodies are constantly bombarded by visceral warning signs, and, in an attempt to control these processes, they often become expert at ignoring their gut feelings and in numbing awareness of what is played out inside. They learn to hide from their selves."
>
> Bessel A. van der Kolk, The Body Keeps the Score: Brain, Mind, and Body in the Healing of Trauma

When force is excessive, it traumatizes us. And, no matter how old we are, we don't learn well, if at all, when suffering the effects of trauma. And in the event the traumatized child does learn, the lessons (outcomes) they take with them are not the ones we intend for them.

I am reminded of a short story written in 1938 by William Carlos Williams called "The Use of Force," which illustrates the dynamic between adult authority and childhood autonomy and the tension between the simultaneous fear that an adult and a child often feel under stressful conditions. In the story, a doctor is making a house call to tend to a girl who is quite sick. Williams was a physician as well as a writer of poetry and short fiction. This experience is likely autobiographical. Williams had likely experienced something similar to that of the narrator, as he too was a medical doctor who made house calls during the diphtheria outbreak in the years of the Great Depression. The narrator in the story comes to the Olsen home to treat their daughter, Matilda, for what he thinks might be diphtheria. The doctor decides to examine her throat. The girl, though, has other ideas and refuses to open her mouth to the doctor, so the doctor and the girl's parents proceed to use significant physical force to restrain her and examine her throat. The reader of this story becomes inevitably uncomfortable with the overwhelming force that the adults use to open her mouth and keep it open. The doctor in the story struggles to look down her throat, but the more force he uses to open her mouth, the more she struggles to keep it closed. Although it is against her self-interest to show him that she has kept the symptoms of diphtheria from her parents and the doctor, she uses as much force as she can muster to resist the doctor. The story is violent. The doctor's anchoring belief is that he knows better what is good for her, and he is right. His intention to help her is pitted against the girl's absolute struggle for autonomy and personal freedom because of her resistance to external forces and her natural fear of death. She does not trust the doctor.

Reminiscent of William James's sarcastic hyperbole in equating teaching to warfare for the teachers in Cambridge, Williams's story tells of the transmutation of adult care into sheer force. The doctor and the girl's father collude to overpower this sick and frightened child's fragile autonomy, annihilating any trust she had in them, a trust necessary for any healthy medical treatment. Her futile and desperate resistance in the face of sheer adult force is an important metaphor for our purposes here. It is very much like the method of teaching that I was trained to use and did use in my first four or five years of teaching, like *old school* and even *new school* attempts at injecting rigorous academic standards into curriculum that are relevant only to the dominant culture, the adult world, and the cultural literacy of the owning class.

> In war, all you have to do is to work your enemy into a position from which the natural obstacles prevent him from escaping if he tries to; then to fall on him in numbers superior to his own, at a moment when you have led him to think you far away; and so, with a minimum of exposure of your own troops, to hack his force to pieces, and take the remainder prisoners.
> William James,
> *Talks to Teachers on Psychology and to Students on Some of Life's Ideals*

Just as Dr. Williams believed that he knew best what was good for his patients, I thought I knew better what was good for my students, and maybe I did, sometimes. And like the doctor, I used my belief that I knew better to justify forcing my students to listen to me, to read, to write, and ultimately to comply with my demands. I called this teaching, and though I didn't realize it until later, I was not only traumatizing my students, but I was preventing them from assimilating the very knowledge I wanted them to learn.

Trauma and Learning

"Force creates unintended and unanticipated consequences when applied to our teaching. I am not saying we shouldn't ever use force, but we should always remember that there is a price to pay for having control."

Dr Robert Cunningham,
Principal of *Shawsheen Technical High School*, from 1984 to 2014

Robert Coles, author, child psychiatrist, and professor, planned to be a teacher while an undergraduate at Harvard in 1950 but became a doctor and psychiatrist instead after meeting the elderly author and doctor, William Carlos Williams, who urged him to consider a career in medicine. Coles met Williams when he interviewed him for his senior thesis, during which they discussed what is lost when teachers force students to learn and when doctors force patients to take treatment. Students who are forced don't learn, and patients who are forced don't heal. It may look like they do, but they are only complying, a pretense used to interrupt and survive the trauma of being forced. Compliance is not learning, nor is it healing. Though he did start his career in psychiatric medicine, eventually Coles became a teacher, and for many years, he was a professor at Harvard.

In his 1989 book, titled *The Call of Stories: Teaching and the Moral Imagination*, he writes,

> When I began teaching college students and medical students, I found those stories powerful in their impact upon those young men and women who, like Williams, struggled with ambitious intelligence as a force that can demolish 'the heart's reasons'--namely, a warm empathy, a considerateness toward others, a willingness, even to let them become one's teachers, however humble or troubled their lives.

When the raw force of intellect serves to "demolish the heart's reasons," we, as teachers, like the doctor in the story, conspire to (and do) traumatize our students.

> ... hold both her wrists.
> But as soon as he did the child let out a scream. Don't, you're hurting me. Let go of my hands. Let them go I tell you. Then she shrieked terrifyingly, hysterically. Stop it! Stop it! You're killing me! Do you think she can stand it, doctor! said the mother. You get out, said the husband to his wife. Do you want her to die of diphtheria? Come on now, hold her, I said.

Then I grasped the child's head with my left hand and tried to get the wooden tongue depressor between her teeth. She fought, with clenched teeth, desperately! But now I also had grown furious - at a child. I tried to hold myself down but I couldn't. I know how to expose a throat for inspection. And I did my best. When finally I got the wooden spatula behind the last teeth and just the point of it into the mouth cavity, she opened up for an instant but before I could see anything she came down again and gripping the wooden blade between her molars she reduced it to splinters before I could get it out again. Aren't you ashamed, the mother yelled at her. Aren't you ashamed to act like that in front of the doctor? Get me a smooth-handled spoon of some sort, I told the mother. We're going through with this.

William Carlos Williams, "The Use of Force"

Trauma is antithetical to learning. It creates impediments to assimilating new knowledge proportional to the depth and breadth of the trauma experienced by the student, whether a child or adult. Children are especially susceptible to suffering from a pathology like trauma that demolishes any chance for students to be intellectually curious enough to learn higher-order thinking skills. Trauma too often has its origins in experiences where our consent is denied, like in cases of extreme emotional and verbal abuse, sexual assault, and also physical assault or being forced to witness these types of violence firsthand. The denial of consent is essentially what defines force and causes trauma. Making the most essential needs, like food, shelter, and love, conditional may be less brutal but is still forceful. Less extreme uses of force like coercion, manipulation, and the threat of withholding personal freedoms or desires can trigger the symptoms of PTSD and contribute to *developmental trauma* in children. Children learn that their personal freedom is not a right but instead a currency, and that love, care, and intimacy are conditional.

My mentor and the principal of the school where I taught for 16 years once explained to me the uncontrollable power of force this way. He said, "Force creates unintended and unanticipated consequences when applied to our teaching. I am not saying we shouldn't ever use force, but we should always remember that there is a price to pay for having control." Certainly, not all force is equally harmful. The less traumatic the force, the less harm. But any level of unnecessary force is an impediment to the long-term education of children, because the consequences for children are that they have trouble forming relationships with teachers. They develop poor self-regulation skills. They adopt habits of negative thinking. They become chronically hypervigilant. They become deterministic, which undermines their intrinsic motivation. Their executive functioning becomes weakened, and their locus of control becomes external. Students who experience trauma regularly over a period of time may even have interrupted development in their prefrontal cortices. This is the part of the brain that regulates impulses, attention, planning, decision-making, and self-awareness.

PTSD is defined in the American Psychological Association's *Diagnostic and Statistical Manual of Mental Disorders* (DSM-5) as a psychological, emotional, and behavioral disorder that occurs after some individuals experience a trauma or traumas such as violence from warfare, sexual assault, child abuse, domestic violence, or some other violent or forceful event or events. Symptoms often include menacing, unwelcome negative thoughts and feelings, or dreams related to the original traumatic events. Such mental and even physical distress interrupts the learning process, especially when trauma-related cues, otherwise known as "triggers," unconsciously change the way we think and feel, increasing our *fight-or-flight response*. These symptoms are difficult to recognize in young children, making it more difficult to prevent them from triggering their PTSD. This is both an emotional and a physiological response for which trauma victims have little control.

The amygdala is a part of our brain, residing deep within the temporal lobes of the cerebrum, known as the central memory processing center, where decision-making and emotional responses are generated. Research shows (Van der Kolk, 2014 & Goleman 1996) that the amygdala is overactive in patients with PTSD. Because the amygdala is where memory is formed in our brains, PTSD becomes an acute liability to the learning process. Learning always involves memory, and when we experience the symptoms of PTSD, we re-experience the trauma that caused it. This re-experience is more than a simple distraction for the learner. Neurologically, it is a stressor on our brains and a memory inhibitor. During the stress of a triggering event, our brains' hippocampuses, which place memories in a context of time and space so we may retrieve them later, is turned off. Therefore, when we experience stimuli that is similar to the initial traumatic event, our bodies perceive the new triggering event as if it were the original traumatic event, because the accuracy of our memory of these events is significantly reduced.

A Different Kind of Teacher

Once I learned about PTSD, I began to recognize many of the clinical symptoms of PTSD in my students and didn't make the connection to my own teaching immediately, but eventually came to realize that I was part of a systematic tradition of teaching that either caused or triggered PTSD in students. When I came to understand that I had become a trigger for their trauma response, I wanted to quit my job. And, since I was a victim of bullying at a young age myself, I was especially disappointed in myself, knowing that I had become an unintentional perpetrator in the experience of my own students. There was a positive reality; however, embedded in that moment, I learned about the nature of force. If I was traumatizing my students by using force, I could change. I could use less force, or maybe even no force, and hopefully prevent or reduce their trauma. I could, at least, try to stop causing trauma responses (triggers) in my students through my style of teaching.

Trauma causes children to suffer from reduced creativity, trouble sleeping, drug and alcohol dependence, mental illness, emotional dependency, weakened decision-making skills, and shortened attention spans. They are also more likely to choose friends and intimate partners who are more likely to be forceful, denying them their consent and not honoring their basic need for freedom. I had been contributing to these problems in my students, but I realized that if I were brave enough to be a different kind of teacher, I could break from a pattern of demanding compliance and using accountability to enforce my control over them to a more humanistic approach.

I learned the hard way that force has consequences, especially in teaching, and many of those consequences do not align with my goals to help students learn. And we know that the exercise of control over students is also not practical for teachers because these consequences are not always visible, and those applications of force that are invisible, no matter how small, are sometimes very negative (Bandura, 1997). It is often very difficult, sometimes even impossible, to anticipate the consequences of forcing students, which belies the very reason why we do it.

When we try to control our students, make them be this way or that, to do this or that, to try hard, to stop behaving a certain way, to fulfill one of the goals we have for them, we often misattribute the antisocial behavior that follows such use of force, not realizing that we are the cause of the resentment that underlies that behavior. And then we are apt to use more force to bring that behavior under control, further subordinating them as the "other," as apart from us. How can our students interpret their own behavior, which does not match the social norms we value, as anything but inferior? The feeling of being inferior not only reduces self-efficacy, which is essential for learning, but it also breeds resentment in an individual, disrupting the trust that is necessary for teachers to build positive relationships with students.

Perhaps it's developmentally appropriate that some students have a relative inability to self-regulate, or because of the rough edges in their ever-changing and uneven psychosocial development, they are compelled to resist our attempts to control them. Is it because they have been the victims of some trauma in the past that we, and perhaps even they, are unaware of, respond to our attempts to refine their behavior (in other words, coerce, manipulate, condition) with a reaction that is even more disruptive and irrational in a classroom setting? Teachers are imperfect and often overwhelmed by the job. We have our own triggers and traumas, and we sometimes fail to correctly attribute our students' reactions as antecedents to our application of force. However subtle our attempts to change our students' behavior may be, their interpretation of our efforts could easily be catastrophic. They may conclude that we do not accept, approve of, or respect their identities and their autonomy, which is detrimental to relationships, community, and their emotional security needs.

It's so hard for us to attribute their disruptive behavior to our forceful attempts to change them because, as teachers, we rarely see ourselves as perpetrators of something so akin to violence as forcing a person to change. Let's be real, though, just for a minute. For better or for worse, that's what we do, consciously and unconsciously. When we take our first job as a teacher, we enter a long tradition of "socializing" children, which is essentially teaching them how to follow social norms. We can call these norms ethics or morals. We can refer to normative behavior as appropriate and respectful, and I am not advocating that teachers cease and desist from teaching children in school to wait their turn, to share with their neighbor, and to be tolerant of other people's differences. Those normative behaviors are central to our cultural values. When we model, affirm, and even intervene in the behavior of our students, we are doing our jobs. I am simply acknowledging that doing our jobs means that it comes with the territory that adolescents, especially, will react defensively when they perceive we are trying to change them. So, what do we do?

A Final Thought

We must be aware of power dynamics in our classrooms, be patient when students become defensive, tolerant when they are aggressive, and forgiving when they try to hurt us. They often do these things because they are triggered. We must smile as much as possible and be honest with ourselves about the force we use, about how we use that force, and what it does. We must use force economically because the maxim *Primum non nocere*, the one doctors take as their Hippocratic Oath, means, "First, do no harm." It must be our pledge too. Harm is trauma. And trauma prevents learning. So, if, in our pursuit of teaching, we use excessive force and our students are harmed, they will not be able to learn. Even on the most practical level, when we are forceful, we are getting in our own way. On the most ethical level, we are doing the wrong thing. Simply put, we must use as little force as is necessary.

· 10 ·

THE PROBLEM WITH "ACADEMIC RIGOR"

"Rigor of beauty is the quest. But how will you find beauty when it is locked in the mind past all remonstrance?"

William Carlos Williams, Paterson

A few years ago, I sat on the strategic planning committee of an urban school district in the city where I work, and as members of the committee discussed curriculum and teaching, the word "rigor" was used a lot. At one point, I asked the other members of the committee what it meant. They thought I was being rhetorical.

"You know what rigor means, John," one person (who knows me fairly well) said from across the table.

"I'm not sure I do."

"Academic rigor, said another person" (who had just met me) saying the word *academic* as if I meant another kind of rigor.

"Right. But what does that mean, *academic rigor?*" I asked again, softly.

"It's about *standards*, said a third person sitting at the table who did not work in schools. He was from the business community. When he said the word "standards," there was a weighted inflection.

"I think it's about more than that," said the first person.

"Standards for teachers and for students," a third voice chimed in.

"It's about the work being challenging enough to prepare students for college, said a fourth person who was neither a teacher nor a school administrator."

The conversation went on for a few more minutes without resolution. The chair of the committee gave me the same look I usually get at those types of meetings. I was a troublemaker.

"John, let's not get too philosophical about this, ok?" Another member, who also knows me and was sitting next to me, pleaded softly for me to let it go, as if I were the one holding onto it. I stifled the urge to ask why I was there. After all, I am a college professor. Am I not supposed to ask the hard questions? Even still, my intention was not to be philosophical, oppositional, or disruptive. I was being practical.

"I think if we are going to write these words into our philosophy and goals, we need to know what they mean. Don't you? I responded. Whenever I hear people use this term, I think of rigor mortis, and I don't think that is what we want to portray, is it? I thought that we were promoting differentiation now," I said, embracing my inner troublemaker.

"We can have both differentiation and standards, said the first person again." I had to stifle a smile and an eye roll.

"If we are going to change the curriculum to meet the unique needs of all the students with their different learning styles (i.e., differentiation), then how can we do that without being flexible, without adapting and changing the curriculum?" I asked.

"We could talk about this for a long time, said the first person, impatient with my questions."

To their credit, the committee did not want to give the wrong impression, so they decided not to use the word rigor in their district's philosophy and goals. But, after that, I was curious. I had heard the word kicking around as edu-speak for a few years. I wondered where it came from, and if there was a consensus about what it meant in education.

More recently, a local school district I am familiar with hired a new principal who, fresh out of his doctoral program, had been using this term frequently with his faculty. When he was asked what it meant, he gave a similarly vague response to the ones I got from the committee. He said it depends on the situation, but the standards are high. When asked to give an example, he said it means high levels of thinking. This is obviously not an example.

Most curriculum directors, principals, and educational consultants I talk with equate rigor with the language that the Massachusetts State Department of Education uses, like "high expectations." I am guessing that it makes me an even bigger troublemaker if I ask, "High" compared to what?

Back when I taught high school English, I asked my students what they thought it meant, and they told me that they thought rigor meant *the kind of schoolwork that was going to be hard*. I asked my students at the university who are studying to be teachers what they thought it meant. They said, "curriculum and instruction that meets a high level of challenge." I think my high school students said the same thing but better.

Honestly, I don't know what any of this means, and I'm a professor of education. I probably should know. But the problem is not with me—at least not this time. I'm not denying that I am a troublemaker, but this time the problem is that we are blindly following those who worship at the alter of rigor.

A Recent History of Academic Rigor

After doing a little looking around for the first usage of this term in academia, I found several books and other publications by a woman named Barbara Blackburn published between 2000 and 2017 that discuss academic rigor, and though she attempts to dispel what she calls the "myths of rigor" in more than one of her books, she too fails to clearly define what the term actually means. Blackburn rejects the idea that academic rigor is about having teachers assign students piles of difficult reading, and she confronts the notion that rigor means being inflexible, hard, strict, stiff, or tough.

She attempts to explain that rigor is about creating an environment in which all students are expected to learn at "high" levels. She goes on to say that in a rigorous classroom, students are supported so they can learn at these high levels, and that the students must demonstrate learning at "high" levels. These are her repetitions. Not mine. I will repeat my earlier question from the committee: "High compared to what, Barbara?"

Blackburn's books discuss Bloom's Taxonomy, the earlier discussed multitiered list of thinking levels, developed by education psychologist Benjamin Bloom in 1956, long held as a framework for high academic standards that teachers ought to use in writing objectives for their lesson plans.

Bloom's Taxonomy certainly ranks levels of thinking and is a valuable resource for thinking about curriculum and instruction. You will get no argument from me about the value of Bloom's taxonomy. So, is rigor just another way of saying "Bloom's Taxonomy?" If it is, then why just not say "Bloom's Taxonomy" instead? If it's not Bloom's Taxonomy, then I still don't know what rigor is. The stiffness, the inflexibility, and the rigidity commonly associated with the word rigor stay with me. I can't quite shake it. Is rigor a new way of repackaging the old back-to-basics argument that says schools fail to teach children what they *need* to know? Is it part of harkening back to Harold Bloom's (no relation to Ben) prescriptivist approach to curriculum? Or, is it like E.D. Hirsch's belief that everyone should know specific facts by specific ages to be "culturally literate?"

Brian Gibbs, a 2021 professor of education at the University of North Carolina-Chapel Hill, notes in an article he wrote for the National Association of Secondary School Principals (NASSP):

> When I visit schools today, as part of university practicum supervision, my education consulting or for some other reason, the concept of rigor appears everywhere. It is increasingly becoming a term used in mission statements, a focus of instruction, and a component of teacher evaluations. When I ask what they mean when they say rigor, educators stumble, often with a long pause, rarely coming up with a clear answer. At the very least, we need to begin a dialogue about what constitutes rigorous instruction.

Ellen Langer (2016) outlines in her book, *The Power of Mindful Learning*, that her research and the research of others debunk the dominant myths about learning that never seem to go away. The very first myth that most of us believe is that "the basics" should be learned so well that they become second nature. She explains that this is not only untrue but also a liability to the learning process. Langer's research shows that people who learn skills mindlessly without question, through excessive repetition yet with limited opportunities for application and contextualization, are less able to adjust to a change related to the application of this knowledge. And, of course, this approach to teaching requires additional force because students naturally resist lessons that are disconnected from their personal reality.

I do believe that teachers should try to teach children to think at high levels. I also believe that children should value hard work. And I do not think that students who are poor, or learning disabled, or who speak limited English should be cheated out of the most interesting and useful skills that schools can teach, but so do a lot of people, including all the teachers I know. They are trying to teach children to create, evaluate, analyze, apply new knowledge, and understand their worlds every day. Is rigor just code for "schools and teachers are so easy that some children do get left behind?" I think it is.

If so, that code does a disservice to those same children who are left behind, because it oversimplifies a complex societal problem, blaming the very teachers who work daily with those children to educate them to the highest standards they can with the time they have. Those teachers work with the neediest children and are the ones who hear the word rigor the most in faculty meetings, at conferences, and in the scholarship on teaching. They are often told that their lessons lack rigor, mostly by people with no teaching experience, people who couldn't define what rigor is, if you asked them.

Is a Lack of "Rigor" the Same as Bad Teaching?

> "I think that many people are absolutely mistaken, naive, concerning the meaning of rigor."
>
> Ira Shor & Paulo Freire (1987), A pedagogy for liberation: Dialogues and transforming education

Some teachers do interpret rigor to mean piling on hard work. Who can blame us? That's what it seems to mean. Besides all the vague circular definitions of rigor floating around the edu-speak-o-sphere, along with the myriad thin denials that rigor means more work or harder work, what are we left to assume?

Children hate the word rigor. Blackburn discusses what children think about rigor in one of her books, basing her findings on a survey she conducted. She describes a complexity of responses from the children surveyed; her conclusions are a muddy pond teeming with loose children's perceptions of rigor, represented as a "complexity," but her discussion of what they think about the term is unclear. Unlike Blackburn, I taught school for 19 years, and I know all my students hated the term.

Let's play a game of true or false, shall we?

It won't count toward your grade. I promise.

True or false: Children learn less from fun and games than they do from rigorously structured activities.

The answer?

FALSE. In fact, Langer's research (2016) shows that children learn more when they are having fun than when so-called "rigorous standards" are imposed on them inflexibly.

Teachers hate the term rigor too. We don't want to hear about rigor anymore. Most of us will admit we don't know what it means, all the while, suspecting that it means we are doing something wrong by not pushing our students hard enough. Using this word typically implies we are not doing our jobs, and it proves nothing more than that people who don't teach love to tell us what to do.

The Case for Maslow Over Bloom

The phrase "Maslow before Bloom" is being used in various education settings to explain how our focus on academic aspects of learning cannot be addressed adequately until students' basic human needs are met. Most teachers did not need a pandemic to make them see that this was already a problem. Perhaps society does, though. Professor Carol Mutch (2021) and her colleague, Sophie Peung, from the University of Auckland, studied teaching during the pandemic and found that the sudden and necessary transition to remote teaching, along with other pandemic-associated challenges made teaching so stressful that both teaching and learning have been significantly disrupted. The introduction of additional, novel, and constantly shifting professional demands for teachers for delivering different, difficult, and experimental styles of instruction, as well as the challenges of maintaining connections with their students and those students' families while caring for their own families, has created an impossible situation in schools all over the world. So problematic is the current state of affairs in education that academic goals have automatically become sidelined as less important than students' basic human needs for food, sleep, emotional safety, physical security, a sense of belonging, a feeling of connection, and a belief in their own self-worth, as well as simple human autonomy. We were all forced to accept that these needs are most important for children during the global pandemic, but now that we have moved beyond crisis mode, I guess children no longer have those needs. Or perhaps those needs simply aren't as visible, so bring the academic rigor back. I contend that these basic human needs have always been more important than our everchanging and always ramped-up, ultra-rigorous academic standards. These basic human needs that Maslow described must come first. They aren't merely important. They are necessary. They are conditional for cognitive growth and a prerequisite to academic learning and the development of new skills. Both Maslow and Bloom wrote that children cannot assimilate challenging and complex concepts, cannot work outside their comfort zone to develop new understandings, and cannot cope with the inevitable failure that is normal in the process of advanced thinking and learning unless they first have their basic needs met.

True or False Round 2

Teachers can instruct students with flexibility while maintaining inflexible—rigid—standards.
Answer
FALSE. *The less flexible we are (or allowed to be) about standards like the Common Core or state standards, the fewer options we have about customizing instructional methods, and the larger our class sizes, the more magnified this problem is.*

The SEL movement and the global pandemic are why Maslow is back on the front page, so to speak. School administrators, boards of education, and academics have a decision to make now. Do we acknowledge that rigor and that standards (both by definition, essentially inflexible and intended to be) are working against the emotional and mental health of children, working against the emotional intelligence of our students, working against the SEL that policymakers, scholars, curriculum directors, and school committees are promoting? The SEL experts, the new SEL standards, and SEL advocates are promoting curriculum that teaches students to be self-aware, to self-monitor their behavior, to have social awareness, to build relationship skills, to practice responsible decision-making, as well as other soft skills that ultimately require a flexible way of thinking, not a rigorous one.

Literacy research does not support the notion of rigor. The scholarship on reading shows that students who are regularly forced to read texts above their ability levels fail to develop the fluency they need to read at high enough speeds to maintain steady growth as readers.

Studies on the teaching of reading find that learning to read advanced texts depends on an automaticity that can only be assimilated through practice with texts that are at lower grade levels than the students' measured abilities.

Therefore, if rigor means that teachers must assign only difficult texts, our students are doomed. And if rigor instead means the inflexible alignment of curriculum to standards, which is different from the overly simplistic idea that teachers should be challenging their students, then our students are still doomed, because teachers need the flexibility to make judgments about what texts they select for students based on what they know about their students' developmental readiness to comprehend those texts.

One of my consulting clients recently asked me how their K-12 curriculum could represent *both* the new SEL standards and the academic rigor of the common core at the same time. My response was a question: *Which is more important to you?* The client did not answer the question, but clearly the rigor was more important to the client. The question is irrelevant. Without having their needs met, children will lack the motivation or even the ability to attempt rigorous academic work.

A Final Thought

Now that my autopsy of rigor is finished, I think we need to find a hole in the ground in which to bury it. I think there might be an empty plot in the cemetery of useless edu-speak somewhere between district determined measures (DDMs) and value-added measures (VAMs). If not, we can stack rigor on top of the formative assessment for results (FAR) cycle and race to the top (RTT) like they do when they run out of space in the cemetary.

Another myth that Langer soundly debunks in her research is the commonly held belief that learning that is fun is not challenging or advanced enough to be worthy of teachers' time and attention. Her research and that of Mihaly Csikszentmihalyi's (1990) shows not only that advanced learning can be found without repetition, rigor, or force, but that it is best taught using fun as part of the instruction. Stewart Brown (2009), psychiatrist and founder of the National Institute for Play, makes it clear through his research that a lack of play, which he calls a play deficit, can lead to antisocial and even violent behavior, which certainly disrupts learning.

· 11 ·

RESPONDING TO FORCE AND FEAR

> *The amygdala in the meantime has decided, Oh no, I've got to do something! It can hijack the rest of the brain if it thinks there is an emergency, and it is designed to be a hair trigger. In other words, better safe than sorry. This has helped immensely in evolution as a survival mechanism, when you are answering the question: Does it eat me or do I eat it? You can't sit around and think about it; you need to have an instantaneous response. That's how our ancestors survived.*
>
> Daniel Goleman, *Emotional intelligence*

When we try to force our students to behave in ways that fulfill our needs, for example, if we chastise them for literally getting out of a line in the hallway while our boss is walking by or for talking while another adult is talking to them, we show them that they are not important. This builds a pool of resentment in them that is not easily drained off. Even more dangerously, force triggers fear. Because when any of us, children or adults, is forced to do something, either with the lightest touch of coercion or through the execution of brute physical force, the fear center in our brains, known as the amygdala, lights up. This cluster of nuclei, located deep within the temporal lobes of our brains, ensures our physical survival through the "default" of automatic behavioral responses. This crude memory processor gets the first, lightning-fast crack at every "decision" we make, through instinctual and emotional memory rather than rational or logical memory. The amygdala is informed by our fear and responsible for regulating our breathing, sweating, and blood pressure, as well as heightening all our senses. It relies on fear and anxiety as chief sources of data rather than on deeper reflexive and logical analyses to make decisions. Our frontal cortices, where our reflective and thoughtful functioning occurs, go offline temporarily as the amygdala turns on. The amygdala is part of what is called the limbic system. This system is informed by emotion and is especially motivated by fear. It is complexly automated and extremely fast. This is a subcortical sensory system concerned only with what it perceives as threats to our survival.

My limbic system might be switched on when I see my boss, an old school stickler for orderliness and tradition, coming down the hall toward my classroom while my students are talking loudly, off topic and horsing around. My amygdala interprets the event as if this is a threat to my survival, making it more likely I will temporarily discard my high-level beliefs about the best environments where adolescents learn. This cluster of nuclei is considered to be highly evolved and has been present in our species for millions of years. It has played a crucial role in our success as an apex species on this planet. Therefore, our brains place the amygdala in the driver's seat. My amygdala knows that my boss hasn't yet approved my reappointment at the end of the year. The amygdala knows that we need food to survive, a job to get money, and that food costs money. The amygdala's job is to make sure we eat. It is a selfish, survival-focused part of our brains, and in a foot race with other parts of the brain, it will beat the rational brain every time. This is the very definition of what it means to be "triggered," and in this circumstance, we are likely to yell at our students to *be quiet!* with an expression of disapproval on our faces, screaming louder than our voices.

And then it is our students' turn to be afraid. Their frontal cortices go dark, and their amygdalas light up. They, too, are triggered. They don't think about us and our bosses, just as we didn't think of them the moment the boss came into view. The amygdala is a selfish little devil. And the students' resentment is automatic, and our relationship with them is dinged, if not dented.

Any time any of us, whether teachers or students, is *forced* to do something, especially something we do not want to do, did not plan to do, or something that reminds us of a painful event, our brains become flooded with the stress hormone cortisol. And if we add another hormone, adrenaline, to our bloodstream, which is also triggered by a perceived threat, the amygdala gets a danger signal, leading to an even more extreme and immediate reaction. This is known as an "amygdala hijacking."

Under these circumstances, our brains are taking orders from the amygdala. The term "amygdala hijacking" was coined by Daniel Goleman in his 1996 book, *Emotional Intelligence*. This is what happens when cortisol and adrenaline mix together in the temporal lobes of the brain. When our brains perceive a threat, our bodies use these hormones quite automatically to escape (run away), freeze, or fight. This is also commonly known as the "fight or flight response." Goleman states that this almond-sized cluster of nuclei takes signals from our emotions to focus our attention urgently on a perceived threat. This allows our bodies to take immediate action without the processing of rational thought getting in the way. One may think of this as the difference between *reacting* and *responding*. Of course, our brains often get it wrong. The brain's perception of threat is often outdated. For example, dark places are not always dangerous, at least not as dangerous as they were 10,000 years ago. People who are different from us are not always a threat to our survival. Although the fear of people who look, act, talk, and dress differently may have served humans 10,000 years ago, when rival tribes might come in the night and attack our families, in 2024, those tribalistic fears do not serve our interests. Our physical programming has a little bit of catching up to do.

The amygdala is also ultrasensitive to perceived social power, making it easier for us to submit to, comply with, and follow the direction of people who assert their personal authority over us. This accounts for the sometimes subtle and sometimes overt physical responses like sweating, dry mouth, weakening in our extremities, increased heart rate, low pressure, and even temporary paralysis we experience when confronted by our bosses or other people who we believe have power over us. When a stressful situation in the classroom causes our amygdalas to wrestle control away from our rational response to stress, our frontal lobes are disabled. Without a functional frontal lobe, we can't think clearly, make rational decisions, or control our responses to stimuli, like what our students say or do. Though Goleman refers to this as the fight or flight response, it should be called the fight, flight, or freeze response. Mammals like us, who have amygdalas that are flooded with cortisol and adrenaline, respond in one of three ways, all of which are related to physical survival. The first response is actually not to fight. It is to freeze. The idea is that a predator may not see us. The second response is to run away, escape, or flee danger. The predator can't eat you, if it can't catch you. But, if the source of the threat can see us and can outrun us, the only option left is to fight or struggle against the forces that we perceive represent an existential threat to us. Goleman (1996) wrote:

> The amygdala in the emotional center sees and hears everything that occurs to us instantaneously and is the trigger point for the fight or flight response. It is the most primitive survival response. If it perceives an emotional emergency, it can take over the rest of the brain before the neo-cortex (the thinking brain) has had time to analyze the signals coming in and decide what to do. That takes a long time in brain time.

Cortisol is a hormone that is like a natural version of the banned and dangerous anabolic steroids that some athletes use as performance enhancers when they feel compelled to perform beyond their natural limits to win. Cortisol prepares us for unusual and abnormal physical tasks, like running for our lives or fighting to the death. It is useful for survival, but for learning, it is an impediment. Adding adrenaline to this mix is like getting an epinephrine chaser injection on top of a shot of anabolic steroids. All our systems—respiratory, cardiac, muscular, metabolic, and sensory-nervous— are stimulated to do battle or retreat. Then, our blood sugar spikes, charging us up like superconductors; our pupils dilate, enhancing our vision, and our airways open, flooding us with the oxygen we need for fighting, running, or other defensive activities. We feel our hearts beat rapidly, we sweat, and our skin becomes extremely sensitive. Our digestive systems may become upset, getting ready to expel unnecessary undigested food in case we need to be light, nimble, and faster on our feet. Our mouths become dry. We won't need to talk or swallow in the fight or the flight. What triggers this response in the brain? Fear.

This is not an ideal state for learning or teaching, and though an *amygdala hijacking* is not a common occurrence, even a brief or minor occurrence of it will make a teacher or a student feel at least irritable, if not downright ill, during the hijacking and then drained and weak afterward. This fear response is not what teachers want to occur in our students' brains while they are in school, but it is often exactly what we set in motion with our own behavior. And the triggers are different for each student. One student who has experienced trauma may be more easily triggered than a student who has not experienced trauma. Such fear as a trigger can be experienced in the moment or exist in our imaginations. When we are being coerced by someone with power over us, we subconsciously imagine how we might be hurt if we do not comply with what we are being pushed into doing. This part of our brains doesn't know the difference between imaginary experience and real scenarios of danger, which is why our overreactions to events sometimes seem to be so irrational.

Make no mistake, the amygdala force equates to "threat." When we are literally forced to do something against our will, we experience it as fear, a threat, and even trauma. The range of force that exists between the lightest of coercive behavior and the brutest of forceful behavior is neither measured nor analyzed by our limbic systems. The threat is all the same to the brain. Whatever the nature of the threat, a physical fear reaction is triggered in our brains, and it may or may not be proportional to the level of the threat. The amygdala hijacking is one of the greatest liabilities to teaching and learning, and it can occur in teachers and students, especially when force is used to make us do something.

The Unintended Consequences of Using Force

Robert Cunningham was not the controlling stickler described earlier. In fact, he had a libertarian style of management. He used force with students and teachers as sparingly as possible. Because he and I were in our doctoral programs at the same time, we used to talk regularly about teaching and learning. It was in one of those discussions that he once told me that "Force creates unintended and unanticipated consequences when applied to our students. I am not saying we shouldn't use force, but we should always remember that there is a price to pay for having control." I have never forgotten the foundational wisdom of those words. I still ponder the far-reaching costs of using force with my students. I still constantly speculate how high the cost may be to me and my students for my need for control. That price tag is likely much higher than the value of any academic outcome in which we so heavily invest. The expense related to using forceful behavior often outweighs any benefits we imagine, so we as teachers must stop and reflect on how we use force, as well as how much force we use and for what purpose we use it. We need to ask ourselves, Why do we pay this high price?

Is it because too often we do not see the whole picture? We often think that we need to control our students when, in fact, we may not. Or do we not need to apply as much force as we think we do to obtain the outcome we desire? I agree with Cunningham that the use of force is sometimes necessary. For example, justice sometimes requires the assertion of our authority. Also, the maintenance of a safe learning environment sometimes necessitates the enforcement of established social norms. However, it seems to be our habit as teachers, formed through a long tradition, to believe that control of students' classroom behavior is more important than our students' personal freedom.

If a teacher, for example, separates a student from the rest of the class, sending them to the main office as a consequence for continually talking when it is not their turn, that student misses the lesson. They may also be embarrassed in front of their peers. They may fear the disapproval of their parents and other adults for not being able to control themselves. They may be confused about why they behaved the way they did. They may even experience shame if this has been a pattern. And shame is a powerful motivator for pathological behavior. There may be a chain reaction of consequences if they are restricted from playing sports or other extracurricular activities as a result of this situation. The team could lose the game. Their grades may be directly affected. This could affect their grade point average (GPA) and their potential to obtain a scholarship for college. They may be late to a part-time job that pays for their car or their phone if they are compelled to go to after-school detention. They may be unable to care for a younger sibling or elderly relative if they have to stay after school, creating conflict at home. Or none of those things may happen, but what will happen, for sure, is that students' relationships with the teacher will be disrupted.

More often than not, the consequences of the force we apply—if we look for them—will show us whether we really needed to use force in that situation. If we reflect on the consequences of the force we use and know it was necessary, we can also see how much force we actually needed to use in that situation and evaluate whether or not we could have used less force to get the same result. Or did we even need "the result" so badly that we were willing to pay for it with the trust and relationship we may lose? But all of this reflection only occurs after the force is applied and the consequences have been realized. Such consequences will be detrimental to your relationships with your students. However, it is entirely possible that the circumstances of such a situation of student noncompliance may require forceful consequences, such as the restriction of a person's personal freedom and the sacrifice of their after-school time. The point here is that it is most practical for us to avoid using force whenever we can, and when we cannot, to reflect on the amount of force we need to apply so that we do not use more than necessary. This calibration of its use will help us avoid the unintended, uncontrollable, unpredictable, and undesirable consequences that the use of force sets into motion, like the disruption of our relationships with our students.

A Final Thought

As teachers, we must attend to a sincere and unflinching reflection of our use of force. Without getting too deeply into the relationship between need and motivation again, I will say this: We have needs, and our students have needs.

And, as Maslow's 1954 seminal work, *Motivation and Personality*, explained, all of us, teachers and students, have a fundamental need to feel safe, autonomous, and independent. This is especially true for adolescents due to the natural and developmentally unstable aspects of their personalities and cognitive and psychological development. That being said, when our need for control is pitted against our students' developmental need for autonomy and their sense of emotional safety, we put ourselves on a collision course with them, which will at the very least interfere with our ability to form the trusting relationships with them that make learning and intellectual growth possible, and at the most, the worst, make it impossible for us to teach and for them to learn. Unless we are aware, reflective, and sensitive and know what triggers our unconscious behaviors, unless we are watchful, sensitive, and take the first steps to be brave enough to accept that we are vulnerable, our students and their thoughts, theories, and ideas will remain hidden from us and from them. The expression of these hidden thoughts, theories, and ideas is essential for the deepest kinds of learning.

· 12 ·

POWER OF BELIEF

> People's beliefs about their abilities have a profound effect on those abilities. Ability is not a fixed property; there is huge variability in how you perform. People who have a sense of self-efficacy bounce back from failure; they approach things in terms of how to handle them rather than worrying about what can go wrong.
>
> Albert Bandura, *Self-efficacy: The exercise of control*

Late one night in 1963, a young Harvard psychologist named Robert Rosenthal whimsically entered his lab and decided to put signs up on the rat cages as a prank on his graduate students. Some signs said that the rats in those cages were smart. And some signs said that the rats in the other cages were dumb, but it was all a lie. Every rat in the lab was an average, run-of-the-mill lab rat; none of them were especially dumb or smart. They were just regular rats.

The next day, Rosenthal told his graduate students who worked in the lab that some of them were going to be assigned smart rats, and some of them were going to get dumb rats. They were told that it was their responsibility to run the rats through a maze and record how well each rat did. The results were dramatic. The rats he said were smart navigated the maze significantly better than the rats he said were dumb, even though all the rats were the same. It seemed that the thoughts in the researchers' heads had changed average rats into smart rats, and the same for the dumb ones. They became even dumber. Rosenthal wanted to publish his findings, but he had trouble finding an academic journal that would consider his paper because the whole thing seemed so far-fetched. What happened to these rats during the experiment? Were the rats telepathic? Could they read the signs that he put on their cages?

They were neither telepathic nor able to read. Instead, Rosenthal discovered that the expectations his students, the researchers, had adopted from the signs he placed on the rats changed the way that each one of them touched the rats during the experiment. Though subtle, these changes in their behavior changed the rats' behavior. The researchers who thought that their rats were smart felt warmly toward those rats, so they handled them more gently than the researchers who had the "dumb" rats. Other studies have shown that handling rats roughly can hurt their performance in the maze test.

Students are Not Rats

Students are not rats. We do not "handle" them, and we don't run them through mazes. We also do not cluster average students into smart, and dumb groups. Or do we?

Wait. What? Do we handle them, run them through mazes, and group them?

Carol Dweck, professor of psychology at Stanford University, explains in her 2006 book *Mindset: The New Psychology of Success* that simply standing farther away from someone or making less eye contact conveys our expectations of them-to them. These effects are subtle, but real. What we believe about people unconsciously affects our behavior and theirs. This is especially true for teachers. Her research and Rosenthal's have both shown that teachers' expectations of their students' intelligence can raise or lower their intelligent quotient (IQ) scores.

Did the rats really get smarter? Are students losing their intelligence when their teachers don't make as much eye contact? Or are these just effects seen in experiments?

University of Pennsylvania psychologist and researcher, Angela Duckworth, (2016) has conducted studies that show, for example, a mother's expectations can influence the drinking behavior of her middle school-aged child and that military trainers who expect cadets to run faster literally cause them to shave seconds off of their best times.

The Belief-Behave-Influence Pattern

What we believe our students can or can't do subconsciously in fact affects our behavior, and when they—also subconsciously—take notice of our behavior, their sensors tune in to what we may or may not believe about them. Children are *extremely* sensitive to nonverbal cues, especially when they are perceiving what adults believe about their abilities. Adolescents are even more perceptive about what adults think about them than children, because they are essentially "identities under construction," constantly searching their immediate environments for feedback about their traits, their qualities, and their characteristics. They are looking for information about who they might be or who they might be able to be. This makes them extremely susceptible to adopting new beliefs based on what they are sensing and what we think about them.

When this *belief-behave-influence pattern* is repeated, we are initiating changes in them. And, when they adopt these beliefs, their behavior immediately begins to change, even though they are often unaware of this whole dynamic. For example, imagine a teacher has two eleventh grade math classes, and in September, that teacher assumes that one group of 17-year-olds is smarter than the other group. By the end of that school year, they will most likely behave—and be—smarter than the other group. Sadly, the others will behave less intelligently, leading to stagnant cognitive growth relative to the other group. This is hard to believe, isn't it? It's not telepathy, but the effect of mere suggestion seems exaggerated, but it is not.

How far can we take this?

These effects are usually very subtle, right? That's what I thought. Then, I heard about *The Batman*. Daniel Kish has no eyeballs. Yet, he rides a bike because of the power of belief. Belief changed his behavior, and his behavior changed him. Or did it give him an extraordinary ability? Daniel had retinoblastoma at 13, so the doctors had to remove his eyes. Retinoblastoma is a cancer of the retina. Yet today, Daniel walks without a cane. And he can ride a bike down a hill in the woods, and he doesn't even think of himself as blind. How is this even possible? Don't people need eyes to see?

Obviously not. Daniel Kish can see without eyeballs, because he "accidentally" developed his own human echolocation system. Yes. Like bats and dolphins. Hence, he is *the Batman*. He did this because of what his mother did not tell him after his eyes were surgically removed. She did not tell him that he was blind. She did not tell him that he had limitations. This made it possible for him to discover that clicking his tongue creates human sonar, giving him the ability to map out his immediate surroundings inside his imagination. I imagine that when the cops came to tell Mrs. Kish that "she shouldn't let her blind kid ride a bike" after he was injured trying to ride it down the city streets, she rebuked them.

"Don't tell me how to raise my son. And don't tell him what he can and cannot do."

"But, lady, he's going to get hurt," I imagine them saying to her.

"Living his life without being able to ride a bicycle? That's not hurting him? His thinking he is dis-abled? That's not hurting him?" I imagine she might have said to them, as they stood at her door, Daniel standing behind her, bleeding, his mangled bike on the floor of their apartment.

He didn't see any limitations because she didn't. Adults are powerful models, and parents are more powerful, but for most of us, our mothers are the most powerful models. If I were one of those police officers, I would have thought, "That kid's mother is negligent."

But, after I learned about Daniel, how Mrs. Kish parented made me wonder. *What does "hurt" mean? What is a dis-ability?* Daniel was injured many times while trying to live an unrestricted life without functioning eyeballs. His perspective is that injury is a natural part of life. His mother did not push him to do this and did not deny that his physical blindness existed. Without instruction, he eventually developed his echolocation so he could live life like someone with eyeballs.

Nobody had to teach Daniel how to see like a bat. He taught himself. What somebody—like his mother—did do was protect his ability to construct, define, and interpret the world. Do we still think that our expectations don't change our students? Still think it's only an effect that occurs in the laboratory? Is *The Batman* just a fluke?

Teacher Expectations

Any system of education, any theory of pedagogy, any "grand national policy" that diminishes the school's role in nurturing its pupils' self-esteem fails at one of its primary functions.

Jerome Bruner, *The culture of education*

A year after Rosenthal did his experiment with the rats, the principal of an elementary school in San Francisco, read about his research in the journal that finally published his findings, *American Scientist*, and she reached out to him. Her name was Lenore Jacobson.

In the article, he mentioned the possibility that a phenomenon similar to the one in his lab with his Harvard students and the rats may be present with teachers and their students. And so, Jacobson and Rosenthal began to collaborate on a research project at her school. This led to a study that was later published in *Psychological Reports* in 1966. Then, in 1968, the findings of Rosenthal & Jacobson (1968a,b) were published as a book titled *Pygmalion in the Classroom*.

Their book described the effects of the teachers' expectations on the first and second grade students in Jacobson's school. Rosenthal and Jacobson hypothesized that if a group of teachers' expectations of their students' ability were manipulated by researchers early on in a learning process, those expectations would affect the behavior of students in such a powerful way that their performance on IQ tests would change. Jacobson guessed that telling some of her teachers that some of their students were "bloomers" would lead to higher levels of IQ test performance. She and Rosenthal also bet that creating low expectations for other students would lower their IQ scores. It turns out, they guessed right.

Why should teachers care about this study?

Rosenthal and Jacobson found that student performance was intertwined with *teacher expectations* in a powerful way. The research they conducted supported their hypothesis that student academic performance can be measurably influenced in a positive or negative way by the expectations of their teachers. Their data showed that the beliefs of one person about another person's ability, accurate or not, can affect the performance of the other person—in this case, children—in school. This is more powerful if the influencing person is an adult. And even more profound if the influencer is a parent or teacher. On top of all that, they found that the younger the children, the greater the effect.

Their study went like this: Students in Jacobson's elementary school were given a fake IQ test. Their teachers were not told the IQ scores. Instead, the teachers in that school were told that 20% of the school *could be* "intellectual bloomers." The researchers chose a group equal to 20% of the school to be the identified bloomers, but those students were not chosen using any scores or other data. They were chosen at random by the researchers. The teachers were then given the names of the randomly selected students, but they told them they were "bloomers." The term "bloomer" was understood to mean that those students might be intellectually gifted. After the school year was over, all the students' IQs were tested again. And all the students in both the experimental and control groups showed a mean gain in IQ. There were six grade levels in that school. 255 students. They all made IQ gains. There are some obvious theories that we could make related to how their teachers' expectations affected their performance. But that's not even the most interesting part.

The first and second grade students in the experimental group, the "bloomer group," showed statistically significant gains in IQ. Their performance on the real IQ test was in the "intellectually gifted" range. Were they intellectually gifted? If so, when did that happen? And how? Aren't cognitively gifted people smart from birth?

Isn't mental giftedness genetic? Isn't it biological? Smart people's brains work better, right?

Rosenthal and Jacobson hypothesized that the teachers in that elementary school subconsciously behaved in ways that encouraged those students identified as "bloomers" academically, so the mere idea that a group of students were talented changed their teacher's behavior, which changed the students' behavior, and the ideas were controlled by belief.

A study done around the same time found that, like the students in Rosenthal and Jacobson's study, teachers are similarly affected by their students. In 1969, Joseph Jenkins and Stanley Deno, then at the University of Minnesota, studied how student behavior and beliefs affect teacher performance. In their study, the students were told to be attentive or inattentive to their teachers' lessons. Jenkins and Deno found that when students were attentive, the teachers displayed stronger teaching skills.

Carol Dweck (2008), a Stanford psychologist, conducted research on student and teacher *mindsets* in educational settings, which has shown how teachers' beliefs about intelligence affect students' performance in the classroom. According to Dweck's theory, each of us sits somewhere on a continuum of belief depending on our implicit views about the basic origins and development of intellectual ability. She calls these *mindsets*, and each of these beliefs affects how we face challenges like failure, change, and negative life circumstances. Dweck's thesis is that there are two opposing and dominant mindsets in most people. There are two mindsets: *growth mindset* and the *fixed mindset*. These groups are distinguished by how we behave as a response to failure.

If someone has a fixed mindset, they believe that their abilities and other people's abilities are innate, and they interpret the cause of their failures and others' failures as a lack of inherent ability. People who have a fixed mindset do not believe that their abilities can change. They often think that they were born with the abilities they have. They also fear failure because they see it as a reminder of how little control they believe they have over their lives. People with a *fixed mindset* will often stop trying if there is any perceived possibility that their efforts will result in failure, thus causing the failure.

People with a *growth mindset* are less likely to quit in the face of failure. They work, even after experiencing setbacks. Growth mindset: people believe that if they invest enough energy, effort, and time, they will likely succeed. People who possess a growth mindset think that their abilities can be developed through effort, assistance from others, and persistence. Dweck's research argues that people with a growth mindset experience less stress in life, and they are also more likely to improve their abilities.

Dweck's theory is similar to early social psychologist Julian Rotter's (1954) theory of locus of control. Rotter's theory holds that some people believe they have control over the outcomes of events in their lives, whereas other people believe that their lives happen to them. Those individuals with what he called an internal locus of control believe the events in their lives are primarily due to their own behavior, their actions, and their effort. Conversely, people with an external locus of control tend to blame their failures or negative circumstances on external forces such as bad luck.

Dweck believes that a powerful, somewhat invisible, teaching strategy that fosters the growth mindset can nurture classroom culture, using a growth mindset language for praising students. According to Dweck (2010), praising the processes, efforts, methods, decisions, and persistence that students use while accomplishing some academic tasks is more beneficial than praising them by telling them that they are smart.

Dweck theorizes that if teachers express to their students the idea that challenging activities are exciting, when they make mistakes and fail, they are more likely to continue to struggle rather than quit. They are also more likely to allow teachers to help them while they struggle, giving teachers the unique opportunity to intervene at important growth points in the learning process.

Dweck's work has identified the importance of using the word "yet" as a powerful way to give students feedback. When students express that they cannot do something, a teacher who interjects "yet" is displaying a *growth mindset*. That teacher's students are more likely to persist and, as a result, more likely to succeed.

When a classroom experience has challenging learning tasks but also includes praise for the process and an explicit growth mindset in teaching language, students will obtain the tools they need to cope with failure and to accept mistakes as temporary, even as part of the learning process.

Like Dweck, Rosenthal and Jacobson concluded that teacher expectations can and do influence student achievement. They believed that the attitude and mood of a teacher could positively affect student performance. They theorized that perhaps teachers give more attention to students they think have special abilities and treat them more warmly when they struggle with challenges. They also guessed that the teachers in the study may have subconsciously behaved in ways (toward the students they thought were "bloomers") that encouraged their success.

Conversely, and as mentioned previously, some studies show that teachers may also be affected by the students in their classroom in much the same way. Our performance may be influenced subconsciously by our students' attitudes, and moods and the behavioral consequences of those moods and attitudes. The potential for a dynamic that I call the *reciprocal expectation effect* may exist in classroom environments where a teacher has faith that his or her students can learn the curriculum, while at the same time, the students believe that the teacher can teach them the curriculum. When this phenomenon occurs, a success spiral bends upward, and the rate, intensity, sustainability, and level of achievement rise continuously as the teacher believes in the students' abilities and the students believe in the teacher's abilities. The only thing stopping this upward spiral is when expectations are countered by doubt, disrupted by fear, or the relationship ends for summer vacation. When a teacher expects a group of students to perform well academically, they are more likely to do so. Once the students start making progress, they are likely to credit the teacher with being a good instructor. The teacher senses that the students expect him or her to be a good instructor, so the teacher is more likely to be good at his or her job, and then the teacher expects the students to be able to perform more challenging academic tasks. And so on. It's quite literally, as they say, "all good."

The importance of the study is that the most subtle behaviors can affect our students' ability to learn, achieve, and become educated. How we look at students, our tone of voice, and our posture all influence their performance and, cumulatively, their ability.

Albert Bandura

Have you ever had a teacher tell you that you were dumb or lazy? How did that affect you? In 1977, Bandura was investigating how modeling helps people who are scared of snakes. During this study, Bandura discovered something about his subjects. He realized that their beliefs about themselves—their beliefs about their own capacities to alleviate their phobia and cope with their fear—changed their behavior and mediated their fear-arousal. He decided to launch a research project to investigate the role that the thoughts we have about ourselves play in our psychological functioning, and as a result, changes in our behavioral patterns.

This became the central theme of his 1977 book, *Self-Efficacy: The Exercise of Control*, and a decade later, his landmark, *Social Foundations of Thought and Action*. From his research on how people's beliefs about their own ability affect their performance, he developed a theory of human functioning, describing how self-regulatory and self-reflective processes are at the center of how humans adapt and change to the conditions they experience. The theory further explained how people are not merely reactive creatures, impulsive, and influenced solely by inner and outer forces. His theory identified self-organization, self-reflection, and self-regulation in subjects as internal behaviors that proactively define our responses to conditions and are embedded in identity. He wrote in 1986:

> Ability is not a fixed property; there is huge variability in how you perform. People who have a sense of self-efficacy bounce back from failure; they approach things in terms of how to handle them rather than worrying about what can go wrong.

This theory, when applied to student motivation and learning outcomes, shows that students' perceptions about their own ability to perform can lead them to set higher goals for themselves because they believe they are capable of accomplishing those goals. This increases the likelihood that the students will try to accomplish those goals. Because effort is almost always required to accomplish academic goals, trying (using energy to make an attempt) makes it possible for them to actually learn. If a child does not believe that his or her efforts will pay off, then the child is not likely to invest the time and expend energy to try for it. They will reach for what they perceive to be the lower-hanging fruit. This is not laziness. It's human nature. We are programmed not to waste our time and energy trying to do things that we believe we are not able to do. It is that simple. Cellular biologists call this theory "homeostasis." And, evolutionary biologists call this the theory of "conservation."

Thus, self-efficacy is about a person's (for our purposes, a student's and/or a teacher's) belief or expectation that participating in specific actions (work, effort, or expending energy) may help them achieve their goals. When the teacher told you that you were lazy or dumb, did that help or hinder your performance in the class? Did those words have an effect on your ability to assimilate new skills in that subject matter even after that school year? Do you still feel you are not good at math, chemistry, or spelling—whatever it is?

In 1985, another psychologist at Harvard, named Irving Kirsch, was studying a similar effect called *the placebo response*. He discovered that expectations play a powerful role in the effectiveness of medical treatment. Kirsch found that when patients think that a treatment will work, displaying a stronger response than thinking the treatment might not work, the treatment is more likely to work, even when the treatment is inert. Kirsch's work and the work of other researchers like neuroscientist Candice Pert reinforce Bandura's *theory of self-efficacy*, showing that our beliefs about what we can and can't do are not imagined. This complex, little understood cognitive process is often described as *the mind-body problem* (Pert, 2010). It enables us to transcend our immediate environments and challenges, giving us access to what seems like a magical power to shape our lives.

Have you ever had a teacher express that they believed in your ability? How did that affect your performance in their class and in that subject? Were you more resilient in the face of setbacks? Were you less afraid to take intellectual risks? Did you expend more effort in that class?

A Final Thought

For teachers, the power of belief is unleashed when we begin to see it, awaken to it, become conscious of it, and make it visible to our students. When we can catch ourselves judging students as being lazy, stupid, or bad, when we are conscious of the beliefs we hold that give birth to those judgments, the ones that influence our own thoughts and behaviors—another example of Bakhtin's "internally persuasive discourse" in action. We possess the potential to change our behavior. We can use conscious and intentional expectation messaging to give our students an advantage. This changes the rules of the game completely because our students' belief in their abilities will be transformed, and consequently, their behavior will as well. Isn't this what *real* teaching is?

· 1 3 ·

ANOTHER WAY

When a teacher asks a question in class and a student responds, she receives not just the "response" but the student. What he says matters, whether it is right or wrong, and she probes gently for clarification, interpretation, contribution. She is not seeking the answer but the involvement of the cared-for.

Nel Noddings, *Caring: A Feminist Approach to Ethics and Moral Education*

We know from cognitive psychology that removing a habitual behavior without replacing it often leads to failure. So, it is important for us as teachers to not only reduce our use of force and fear with our students, but to actively replace it with new behaviors, intentions, and goals that will become the habits of our new way of teaching. The following are some of the mindsets, guidelines, and commitments I do my best to implement in place of using force in my teaching. Most importantly, and for the most practical, and at the same time, the most ethical reasons, fear must be replaced by *trust*. Because learning is a deeply personal, internal, and vulnerable process, leaving each of us fragile and exposed, as a teacher, I have found that building some level— any level—of *trust* is essential for the teacher-student relationship. I found that if my students do not trust me to keep my word, to follow through on my promises, to protect them from harm when they are with me, to see them as individual human beings, and to be relatively consistent, direct, and clear about my expectations of them, our work will be no more than a superficial exercise, and their behavior will be nothing more than the consequences of my coercion.

During my 30 years of teaching, I have learned how precious, fragile, and vital *trust* is. And developing even the most modest of trust with each student starts with how I see them, what I believe about them, the language I use in our communications, and the mindset that guides my decisions relative to them. Like good parents, teachers care about their students beyond any academic or vocational lessons, beyond the realm of school, and even beyond the years we have with them. We hope to fulfill their needs as much as we can, to consider them equal in human value, and to teach them life as an art, but only if they show they want to learn it. Although no teacher should work for a school district or other entity without a contract, a salary, or benefits, our relationship with students must be understood as unconditional. Rules, lectures, and other modes of instruction must be imparted as free knowledge, as if we were helping our own children grow and navigate the world. In order to convey this precious spirit of trust, this energy of intimacy, and this essential confidence in care, teachers must be bound to their students by a commitment beyond that of any legal or social contract. Without this sacred promise, students will not know what our motives are. *Trust* comes not from our statements but from the consistency of our behavior, from our responses to the tests they have for us, and from the patient care that transcends strategy, method, or curricula. Only one's ethos will be sensed by students, whether they are young or old.

Though this commitment sounds heavy, all that is required is that we put their interests and well-being first and that we only do what we know they will benefit from. We are not perfect, but if we, through the best of our ability and judgment, do no harm or injustice to them, their trust in us will be internalized. And no practical person believes that we are immune from mistakes, so harm may come to them even because of our unintentional decisions. However, as long as once we know we have caused them harm, we acknowledge our error, accept our own imperfection, and apologize to them, distrust will not only be avoided, but the level of trust may be deepened.

Reflect on how we interact with students

Just as doctors in their oath promise not to "give a lethal drug to anyone if they are asked," teachers will not use any harmful pedagogy nor prescribe any dangerous curricula, even if our colleagues are doing so or our principals are directing us to do as such. We do not need to force students through coercion, conditioning, or the threat of punishment to accomplish our objectives as long as they are pure and carried out authentically in our daily lives, as if we were artists. We must move forward only for their benefit, avoiding all acts of impropriety or corruption that violate the fragility of our intimacy with them, despite any allure of ego or control. Although we legally cannot keep all information about them secret, we can, whenever possible, maintain their privacy by not discussing their issues, actions, and behaviors unless legally required to do so, especially if the discussion is about anything that is critical of them as learners or people. I have found that I am more supportive of my students when I consistently ask myself:

- How do I see them?
- What do I believe about them?
- What can I expect from them?
- What do I say to them?
- What do I say about them?
- How do I behave with them?
- How do I make decisions about them?

These questions help me to be reflective, *mindful*, and caring as I relate to my students, because understanding how I relate to them and how they perceive our interactions makes me a better teacher.

Establish positive relationships with students

Compliance-based education is so embedded in the culture of teaching that we must actively work to replace power relationships between students and teachers with ones of mutual respect. This is accomplished in the same way that we build all positive relationships with friends, relatives, and colleagues. Though our students are not our family or our colleagues, and we cannot have the same intimacy with them as we do with our friends and family, this takes time, trust, and the explicit expression of support and care. I did, in fact, love my students when I was a classroom teacher, and I still do now. That was not always true. At one time, I feared my students too much to love them, but once I surrendered myself to the idea that I wanted them to be happy, wanted good things for them, that I cared about them, accepted the fact that they could and would hurt me, and that I would heal from that, I was able to love them. All at once and over the years, that love transformed my teaching.

The best way I learned to establish a positive relationship with a new group of students is to greet them at the door at the beginning of class, make eye contact with each of them, be present enough to see them, and notice how they are at that moment. After I left classroom teaching for academia, I came across a study published in the *Journal of Positive Behavior Interventions* by Clayton Cook et al. (2018). They found that teachers who invest their time on the front end, greeting students every day at the door to their classrooms, save more time on the back end because they spend less time responding to problematic behavior and more time teaching. The reason, the authors conclude, why this works is that those teachers who use positive greetings at the door each day avoid reacting to disruptive student behavior by publicly reprimanding and/or otherwise punishing them, which negatively affects their relationships with students. Such regular, mindful, and positive interaction with students, however brief, prevents disruptions, therefore preventing the teacher from responding in a negative way that would contribute to a negative classroom culture. Students are more likely to feel seen, feel safer, and relate to teachers who notice them and the various states they find themselves in throughout adolescence.

Build community in our classrooms

This starts with thinking and talking about our classes as made up of individuals. Instead of thinking about my classes as a *me* and *them* paradigm, I learned to reframe my idea of what *we* do as a group effort, a communal journey, or a family business. If you change your perspective on your classes in this way, adding a new level of care and respect to the dynamic, thinking of *us* and *we* instead of you and me, will focus everyone on the group. Your goals will be shared goals, and you will *all be in this together*. The ownership of the learning time and space as well as the responsibility for decision-making can be shared, creating equity and modeling fairness. This promotes listening and normalizes feedback. Members of the class will support one another's individual and group goals. This requires a sharing of authority and a letting go of control, so as you let go, start small and build toward *communitas*; otherwise, your students may misuse the authority that you give them.

Deepen your teaching toolbox

We will have no reason to put away *the golden hammer* and reduce our use of praise, reinforcement, conditioning, shame, and manipulation if we do not have new ways of being with our students. In fact, our hammers are often invisible because they are culturally acceptable and shrouded in tradition; they become automatic. As Don Miguel Ruiz (2011) says in *The Four Agreements*, we become "auto-domesticated animals." We even turn the hammer on ourselves, unnecessarily punishing and rewarding ourselves, out of socialization and habit. Cooperative learning, inquiry-based learning, game-based learning, experiential learning, dialogic learning, critical pedagogies, narrative paradigms and constructivist approaches are just some of the tools we can employ in place of the hammer.

Teach social and emotional skills as part of our curriculum

Because trust, care, and empathy are essential for people to learn when working in groups, we must model the self-regulation, self-awareness, grit, and the vulnerability that are required for people to work together. Collaboration and cooperation are important in school and even more important after school is all over, and it takes time to teach—years. If we rush our teaching or force people to work together, we do more harm than good, so as we do so, we must be gradual and reflective. If we explicitly teach social and emotional skills like how to be aware of others' needs, how to set boundaries in relationships, and how to appropriately express emotions, we can reduce conflict and, at the same time, improve academic outcomes. However, if we add this to our explicit teaching and consistently model these behaviors, the chances that our students will be able to apply those lessons will increase significantly.

Focus our pedagogy on our students' needs

If we focus more on knowing what students need than on accomplishing the goals of a standards-based agenda, we will build trust. If we focus more on meeting those needs than on creating the appearance of order in our classrooms, we will be able to build a positive learning community. If we choose to focus more on supporting our students than on external perceptions of success as teachers, like test scores, our students will intuit an *ethic of care* that will motivate them to work with us instead of against us or follow directions simply out of compliance. They will ask for help when they need it, and they will not be afraid to show us when they don't know something. They will also take the academic risks that are necessary for intellectual growth.

Encourage students to ask for help

For generations, people working in schools have consciously and unconsciously reinforced the belief that asking for help is a sign of weakness, which belies the very reason teachers are in schools. If we are not working with students to help them learn, then why are we there? Again, the best way to do this is through modeling. If students see *us* asking for help, they will do the same. When I was a schoolteacher, I frequently asked my students for help. There were many things they were better at than I was. Using computers is a good example. Because my students were digital natives and I am a digital immigrant, asking for their help was not merely a means of modeling the behavior I wanted them to emulate. The "ask" was authentic, and they understood that I was being vulnerable by admitting I did not know how to do something. For example, our school's Internet system had a firewall that did not permit us to access YouTube in the classroom. So, one day when, I wanted to show my students a video clip of Mel Gibson playing the role of *Hamlet*, I asked them how I could "hack" around the school's firewall. After a brief period of apprehension, two students who were in our schools' Internet Technology Program showed me a "backdoor" that allowed me access to YouTube. It worked, and we watched the clip without any discussion of how I had engaged students to help me violate the the school's internet security. After moments like that, our relationship deepened, but not merely because our minor collusion made me vulnerable. It was also because I had admitted that I did not know something that they knew.

Be conscious of the limiting beliefs

Instead of projecting to our students that there is a dualism of right and wrong answers about the world, let them express their questions and their theories without judging them, and ask them why they think what they think, rewarding their thinking rather than their "rightness," because teaching students to think is more important than teaching them to be right. One example of where to start with this is to establish *classroom norms* collaboratively with our students and revisit those norms whenever necessary. Creating and revising class expectations with my students instead of writing them on my own before meeting them helped to develop an ethos of "we" rather than an unnecessary *dual-fold consciousness* of I and Thou. This was often the very first collaboration I would enter into with my students each year, showing them that they had shared ownership of "our" class and that they were the owners of their education.

Invest in classroom culture

Management guru, Peter Drucker, is credited with the quotation, "Culture eats strategy for breakfast." Whether Drucker coined this phrase or not, its genius lies in the fact that, as a maxim of organizational structure, performance can be increased by the power of group consciousness, or ethos. The omnipotence that culture holds over individual teaching methods, strategies, or best practices to motivate people toward a goal is significant. This is due to the self-reinforcing character of culture. Instead of "managing students," as most teachers try to do, using what they call "best practices," teachers who intentionally work to build culture with their students use less surveillance, fewer incentives, and practically no punishments. Because conditioning undermines autonomy and independence, we must replace our need for control by collaborating on an imperfect but authentic classroom culture where students' intrinsic motivation is valued over extracting compliance through carrots and sticks.

Commit to doing the same tasks that we assign students

Alexander the Great, son of King Philip II of Macedonia, educated by Aristotle and inspired by Homer's epic heroes, became king at the age of 20, after his father was assassinated. Why do I bring him up here? I do so because Alexander commanded a relatively and intentionally small yet more powerful, skilled, and loyal army than his enemies. Although they were also underpaid regularly risked their lives for him, they adored him. Why? Alexander wore the same uniforms his soldiers wore. He trained hard with them. He led from the front when in battle, where he too was vulnerable, and he ate with his troops, slept with them, and showed great affection for them. As a classroom teacher, I did the same as often and with as much heart as I could. I promised every new group of students I met at the start of every school year that I would not ask them to do an assignment, read a text, write a paper, or take a test that I had not done or would not be doing alongside them, and I kept my word, which was often exhausting but always yielded me two very special boons. The first being that, like Alexander's soldiers, my students loved and respected me. They were loyal to me, and they would perform tasks that were difficult when I asked them to. The second boon is less obvious and romantic, but just as important. By doing the assignments that I required them to do, I experienced those tasks with them, building community and teaching me exactly how hard those tasks were. Sometimes I would come into class after being up late reading a text and admit to them that the reading assignment was just too much. I would apologize, give them the next night off and be more intentional about the workload I put on them.

Listen to students

When I listened to my students, their words, what was behind those words, and what their behavior told me, I not only learned how best to help them but also how not to alienate them. I learned what they liked and wanted, what interested them, and what scared them. Listening to students is not always easy. They do not always get right to the point. They are often probing the boundaries of their autonomy, and sometimes adolescents behave in disrespectful, disruptive, and even hurtful ways. However, whether we are listening to their seemingly irrelevant stories or observing their antisocial behavior, what they say and do communicates their needs to us. We will not be able to untangle our intolerance from their expression of pain, confusion, or need if we don't intentionally look beneath the surface of their statements and under the facade of their actions. So much of what they tell us is inappropriate and angry, but often what they truly want us to know is that they are wounded, scared, and confused. Without seeing through the fog that their fragile egos hide behind and the curtains of our own defensiveness, we will not hear them or be able to help them. And, without hearing their true thoughts and feelings or helping them through the real challenges of growing up, learning is just going through the motions for them as much as teaching is for us.

Do not demonize failure

As Jessica Lahey writes in her 2015 book *The Gift of Failure*, failure is often characterized as a negative in schools; for example, a grade of an "F" is a bad thing. But unfortunately, out of love and care, we overprotect children from making mistakes, when those mistakes are an important part of their development. Caring is important, but protecting children from failure can easily erode that child's confidence, undermine their motivation, and place their ability to construct new knowledge independently at risk.

Disappointment, rejection, and criticism are all invitations for students to learn, but they must be allowed to feel these emotions for them to signal action. Feeling uncomfortable, sad, or angry while grappling with authentic failure can strengthen a student's "grittiness," helping them build the resilience they need to take on challenges and tolerate the setbacks that are normal when attempting to achieve significant goals. Failure builds emotional intelligence by providing students with the opportunity to practice coping skills. If we characterize failure, errors, and poor choices as essentially bad, then we potentially rob them of the chance to set higher goals, take on greater challenges, and accomplish truly amazing things. Without grit, they will not be able to delay gratification long enough to realize longer-term goals. What's the point of reducing the compliance-based education paradigm and bolstering our students' autonomy if they aren't able to tolerate challenges or are not going to strive for greatness?

Encourage play as a part of learning

Although play is commonly associated with immature, juvenile behavior, and childish activities, it is a necessary part of the development of higher-cognitive functions, and it has deep roots in the kind of intrinsic motivation that makes learning automatic and sustainable. Prominent psychologists, including Jean Piaget, William James, Sigmund Freud, W.D. Winnocott, Carl Jung, and Lev Vygotsky, studied the necessity of play in learning and concluded that it is not at all frivolous, and in fact, play is an important part of the learning process. Children and adults who consider an activity as play can more easily focus on objectives and goals and take on difficult challenges than when they understand the same activity as work. Play is an important tool in developing and advancing cognition. It also promotes physical development, which is not separate from intellectual growth. It is essential for the learning of social and emotional skills. Play also promotes healthy relationships at home and in school that are necessary for learning, and neuroscience research shows the important link between role play and the growth of neurons in the brain. Studies indicate that play increases the coping skills that help children process stressful situations. It promotes self-regulation and adaptive functioning.

Research shows that as little as 10 minutes of play per day can improve cognitive abilities in children. These researchers found that playing video games is one of the most common mediums of play for children and adults today. Even playing video games is positively associated with some skills that are strongly correlated with academic success (Hollis, 2014). For example, one study showed that time management, attention span, executive control, memory, and spatial abilities all increased for children playing video games in moderation.

Play can also influence one's social development and social interactions. Much of the research focuses on the influence play has on child social development. There are different forms of play that research has found are likely to influence a child's social development. One study conducted by Sullivan (2003) explores the influence of playing styles with mothers versus playing styles with fathers and how these various styles influence a child's social development in distinct and important ways. This research shows that play is essential for the healthy development of a child's "social competence." The researchers found that children use play to expand their ability to regulate their own emotions and adjust their behaviors in various social contexts. This expansion of social skills in early childhood is an important part of their cognitive development, as their emotional and thinking skills develop interdependently. Also, the interpersonal skills required for learning to build relationships with peers are increased by play experiences, just as they are reduced when a child suffers from play deficits. Another benefit of play is the reduction of anxiety in children. Because children do not learn effectively when they are anxious, the role of play as an antidote for axiety in the learning process is important.

During a child's planning, experimentation, and construction of play, they have the opportunity to interact with peers and to think critically about what works and what does not. They are more likely to observe their own mental processes during play, teaching them both metacognition and *mindfulness* naturally. Before and after play, children are more likely to express their plans and discuss them with their peers. Play promotes love, risk-taking, a sense of joy, enhanced engagement with the world, and enriched self-reflection. Play is often self-initiated and self-directed and is necessary for normal psychosocial development, according to Stuart Brown (2010), author of *Play: How It Shapes the Brain, Opens the Imagination, and Invigorates the Soul*. Brown believes that play behavior is one of the most important parts of being human. It is also part of the development of the natural instincts children must obtain for their healthy psychological development.

Express our curiosity about what our students think

I found that many of my students had lost any intellectual curiosity they may have had as children. Years of compliance-based schooling had scrubbed the natural wonder and inquiry children have out of them. Curiosity is necessary for learning. It is the ultimate key to intrinsic motivation. It stimulates all of us to investigate why things are the way they are, who we are, and what makes other people tick. Instead of using force to "make" my students learn, instead of baiting them or threatening them to perform tasks, I taught them to be curious, to follow rabbits down holes, and to seek the adventure that learning can be. I did this by showing my own curiosity, taking an interest, and asking questions about them, their lives, and their interests. This helped me build relationships, build community, and build trust with them, but it *also* modeled the qualities of wonder, curiosity, and inquiry.

Assume students want to learn even the most difficult skills

Learning is beyond entertaining. It is at the very least extremely mentally and emotionally, sometimes physically and socially stimulating, and it is often empowering. At most, it helps all of us, children included, to transcend both perceived and actual boundaries that constrict us psychologically, socially, politically, physically, cognitively, emotionally, and spiritually. Who wouldn't want that? So, why do we need to motivate students to learn? It's because our approach is outdated. It is forceful and requires compliance at every turn. If we, instead, start every day with the assumption that our students *want* to learn and expect that they will enjoy learning, we will behave differently, and so will they.

Cultivating habits of curiosity through modeling

Encouraging a love of learning and autonomous action in the culture of our classes, we must gradually replace the idea of learning as work with the idea of learning as play. Curiosity arises out of inquiry, starting with a question. Children are naturally curious. We don't need to teach them to have questions. We merely have to take advantage of the curiosity that is already present by using inquiry-based learning. And we need to resist the urge to restrict, redirect, and reframe their questions. When we do this, we are discouraging them from asking, signaling that their curiosity is irritating. Oftentimes, we do not even need to cultivate curiosity. Instead, we merely have to honor it.

Guide students instead of controlling them

We must replace our need for control with a spirit of guidance. To obtain independence regarding any skill, learners must be set free to make bad choices, mistakes, and errors and to go off course. These are natural aspects of the learning process. Guidance is important for all of us as we learn, but American schooling has a bad habit that we must break if we want students to reach skill levels for literacy, creativity, problem-solving, and critical and analytical thinking that are at an independent level. This reaches beyond our fear of their failure. Our need for control treats their education as a means to serve our ends. The goals, objectives, and standards—whatever you want to call them—that we have set for students in schools are designed to serve our economic needs. They are not designed with the needs of today's learners in mind. The ways in which we attempt to help them accomplish "our" goals are controlling, manipulative, and forceful. We use the same methods of conditioning for them that we use for horses, dogs, and any other animal we wish to domesticate. Grading systems, high-stakes testing, and various rating systems, beyond being flawed in their validity, only serve to reinforce our control over them. This does not "breed" autonomy. The consequence is dependence. We must stop rewarding behaviors that guide students toward predetermined academic outcomes that are set without their consent or even their knowledge, and we must resist the allure of using competition to motivate students to behave as we want them to. Because competition is useful in the capitalist marketplace, captains of industry with little knowledge of learning theory or education research have for decades used their political influence to shape education policy and practice, promoting competition as their way to push students toward the mastery of skills that they think they need in their future employees. But when I look at my students, I do not see future workers. I see people with hopes and dreams, with wounds and fears, with history, and with their own futures.

Competition has significant limitations in K-12 classrooms, and it can be a serious liability to students. In his 1992 book, *No Contest: The Case Against Competition*, Alfie Kohn explains that competition does little to motivate children to learn. It can even harm the self-esteem they need throughout the learning process. Kohn also points out that competition can be toxic to both relationships and the lessons we teach children about relationships.

Reinforcing the win/lose concept of the *zero-sum game* creates either or thinking, an unhealthy and unnatural dualism that places limitations on our imaginations, on our vision of the world, and on what could be. Children ought to have the chance to make their own way without our systematically placing limitations on them. Cooperative, collaborative, and inquiry-based models are far more effective at placing teachers in the role of guides than outcomes-based schemes.

Embed true-to-life scenarios in curricula

If there are ever times when students are unable to see for themselves why a lesson is or could be important or useful to them, the curriculum needs to be revised. It should be obvious. When I taught high school English, sometimes the students would ask me, "When would we ever need *this* in the real world?" Like most teachers, I dreaded those moments, and for obvious reasons. I felt that I had failed to make the lesson relevant to my students, which was irrational and indefensible. But there was more to it than that, really. I felt trapped. I was part of an education system that required us to teach students only outdated, standardized content that could be measured by standardized tests. The educational standards were set by people who neither knew nor cared about my students. It was difficult for me to explain to them why those lessons were important. Whenever I found that my students could not readily apply what I was trying to teach them in their present or future lives, I knew it was time to ignore the system that did not know them, ignore the high-stakes testing that did not validly assess what they learned, take them on field trips, initiate project-based learning units, invite guest speakers into our class, and gamify our curriculum. If a lesson was not inherently relevant to their lives, then I had to question it, too.

A Final Thought

Other Things to Try:

- Take advantage of teachable moments.
- Teach students, both individually and as a group, how to set their own learning agendas.
- Ask students to assist us when we create rubrics.
- Affirm effort over achievement.
- Vary your instructional models frequently.
- Encourage our students to give us feedback on our teaching.
- Use authentic assessments instead of tests geared toward standards-based education.
- Regularly, hold "class meetings" to allow students to freely express their opinions about the management of the class and the curriculum.

· 1 4 ·

THE TEACHABLE MOMENT

A developmental task is a task which is learned at a specific point and which makes achievement of succeeding tasks possible. When the timing is right, the ability to learn a particular task will be possible. This is referred to as a "teachable moment."[1] *It is important to keep in mind that unless the time is right, learning will not occur.*

Robert Havighurst, *Human Development and Education*

Whether we are learning on the job from a mentor, learning to play a sport or musical instrument from a coach, or learning in school from a traditional schoolteacher, the idea of the teachable moment is a feature of the learning process that seems ubiquitous yet whose definition is elusive. I was a schoolteacher for nearly two decades, and now I teach teachers at the university level. I have used this term many times, often regarding it as a universal term that everyone knows. Recently, I realized that it has been a large part of my teaching method for a long time, even though I have never consciously analyzed what it means, how it works, and how it stands in comparison to other terms in today's lexicon of teaching.

Where does the term come from?

The term was first used in a short book published in 1905 in Boston by a little-known author named Walter E. Brandenburg. The book was called *The Philosophy of Christian Being*. And on page 84, he used these two words, teachable and moment, together to imply that a learner has the potential to be especially ready to learn a lesson about something significant and even difficult. And although page 84 of Brandenburg's book was describing the learning of a religious experience, the connotation that he lent these two words when used together has become the foundation for what is implied every time these words are used together. Peter Lawson and Susan Flock at Case Western Reserve are among the few who have researched the efficacy of *the teachable moment* as pedagogy. Their 2009 investigation into how teachable moments may be used to assist clinicians in changing patient behavior found that the teachable moments have the potential to reduce unhealthy behaviors like smoking, but they also state that as a concept, this phenomenon remains mostly unstudied, despite its potential for powerful results.

What is a Teachable Moment?

Teachable moments cannot be planned because they are inherently spontaneous. However, teachers can plan for them, which is what I have been doing for a number of years now. Teachable moments are sudden, advantageously educational occurrences arising due to the circumstances of everyday life. And the trainer, coach, or schoolteacher can take advantage of such circumstances because these moments focus the learner in a poignantly relevant way to understand the nature of what is happening and what can be gleaned from it. These moments often do not fit with what the teacher has planned, but teachers like me set aside plans to use such a moment because teaching and learning come easy in this space.

For the teacher who knows how to use teachable moments, it is not his or her responsibility to change the learner or convince the learner of anything, but instead to point at the phenomenon that is (all by itself) instructive, to be present for questions from the learner, and to support the learner as he or she interprets the situation.

Can a teacher make a moment teachable?

A teacher may set out to create the conditions for the teachable moment to occur, but this usually fails because, for example, creating a problem just to have a student solve it violates the authenticity that makes these moments powerful. It is essentially the spontaneous quality of these real-life circumstances that focuses the learner, making the lesson relevant and meaningful. As the Italian education philosopher, Maria Montessori (1959) wrote in her book, *The Absorbent Mind*, good teachers know that their students must be set free to choose their own futures, and we must not interrupt their spontaneous curiosity. "No work may be imposed - no threats, no rewards, no punishments. The teacher must be quiet and passive, waiting patiently and almost withdrawing herself from the scene, so as to efface her own personality and thus allow plenty of room for the child's spirit to expand." (p.240)

And, as Slingerland (2015) wrote in his *Trying Not to Try*, when we finally learn to let go, achieving a deeper sense of spontaneity, we enter *the flow state*, giving off irresistibly positive energy, creating a cascade of potentiality and superpower-like insight and charisma, and attracting powerful personalities and ideas at the same time.

Once, I caught four eleventh graders plagiarizing information from a source on the internet for an essay they were assigned to write in our class. The source they copied from wasn't even very credible. Although I had been trained to punish this kind of thing, I decided not to, even though they were technically cheating. Instead, I taught the whole class how to identify the level of *credibility* a particular source might have. I also taught them where to look for credible sources and how to cite them. I explained that the difference between a disgraced cheater and a successful scholar is sometimes a simple citation. Instead of punishing them for copying information that was not theirs, I believed that I had at least given them the opportunity to cheat, if not set them up for it. A month later, I caught two of them doing it again and decided to punish them. But the other two cheaters learned to ask for help, to cite sources, and even to find credible sources to answer questions they had. The whole class cheated less after that and were better researchers, in part because I made this incident of cheating into a lesson.

Often, failure, error, and even trauma become fertile ground for *teachable moments*. Sometimes people refer to these as "cautionary tales." These are traumatic events, mistakes, or accidents that can be especially instructive because they are memorable, and therefore the learner wishes to avoid them in the future. In fact, one of the distinguishing features of the *teachable moment* is that it is deeply personal and often associated with vulnerability. Having used the *teachable moment* for many years as a teaching tool, I have to say that the more personal the circumstance, the deeper the understanding can be for the student. This takes guts, because most teachers do not want to risk making themselves or their students vulnerable, but if done right, it can be the basis for real progress.

The idea of the *teachable moment* gained popularity in 1952 when an educational theorist named Robert Havighurst wrote about the importance of the moment of readiness in his book *Human Development and Education*. In the book, he focused on the idea of timing our lessons with the readiness of our students. This is an elegant yet fragile synchronicity that he believed was required for our understanding of new concepts and ideas.

Are there any teaching methods that are like the teachable moment?

Case-study analysis, often used in medical and law schools, is a nod toward the teachable moment. Medical and law students study real-life stories from those fields, and because they are authentic and sometimes result in a significant change in, or even mark the end of, a person's life, the students' attention is heightened. It's not until first-year residents have to treat real-life patients with real diseases that the teachable moment is used as a method. Those medical students know that if they make a mistake, it could (sometimrs does) cost the patient his or her life. The medical school professor doesn't tell his or her first-year residents *Class, today we are going to learn about the shingles*. Instead, the professor uses each patient in that hospital as a case and each moment as an opportunity to teach. If, for example, a patient presents with the symptoms of a blood disorder, then the lesson for the day is blood disorders, not shingles.

I taught at a vocational high school where my colleagues who taught in the shops used real people's cars or computers that needed repair to teach students the skills they needed to be successful in their fields. One year, the students there rebuilt the engine in my 1988 Jeep Cherokee. They bored out the cylinders and replaced the 216,000-mile-old pistons that were bleeding oil with new, oversized pistons. It took them a while to do this, but when they were done, I drove the Jeep home. They understood that if they made a mistake, their English teacher's car could be unsafe or simply wouldn't start. Their mechanics teacher didn't say, *Today we are going to learn about brakes*, because that's not what my car needed. They did a brake job the week after on my friend's car, though, so they did get the lesson on brakes—don't worry.

Those students didn't learn how to rebuild an engine or replace brake pads and rotors from a book or lecture. They learned it from doing the work under the supervision of a teacher. This is often called experiential learning, popularized by John Dewey, David Kolb, Kurt Lewin, Peter Senge, and Jean-Paul Piaget.

More on Learning from failure

Nowadays, part of my job is to supervise student teachers in what the university calls *practicum*, where they practice-teach for 14 weeks in a real school in a real classroom with real students. My students are naturally anxious before they begin their first day in the role of teacher. I try to reassure them that they are ready, but I don't tell them, *Don't worry, the students won't bite, because you never know.* In fact, I did have a student who was bit once by one of her students. She was not one of my student-teachers, but she sure learned a lot from that moment. It's the authenticity that makes case studies, grand rounds, autoshops, student teaching practicums, and various lab settings effective for teaching skills that are important. Ultimately, it is when my students make mistakes during their student teaching practicums that they learn the most.

Why? These mistakes are indelibly memorable because they place the student in a vulnerable position. Making mistakes with real people in real classrooms has real consequences for my students, and the students they are teaching. It is important that afterward, they have an opportunity to reflect deeply on what happened and to consciously evaluate all their options before making their next decision. When they discover such a mistake, they can learn that they must own it that people are not perfect. And, most importantly, any one of my student-teachers who simply forgets one of their students' names, gets angry and yells at a whole class, or chooses material that is too difficult for their students, causing them to fail, can take the lessons they learned from those moments and carry them forward into every class they teach in the future, not as a burden but as a reminder that they will make mistakes, learn from them, and move on.

They learn to expect their students to make mistakes and to teach them to capitalize on those mistakes, so they can get the same benefit; therefore, they learn that when they become professional teachers, they do not want to punish error but instead help their students reflect on it. They might even—as I do—model how I learn from my failures by talking about mistakes I have made openly. Verbally unpacking what I learned from them and how I learned from them.

As a former high school English teacher turned university professor, I often irreverently refer to my new home as "Teacher School," and I sometimes find myself thinking about how academics in teacher school teach students how to teach. This leads me to question the efficacy of the current trend of identifying learning objectives, of backward planning, and of scripting learning activities in light of what I know about the power of the teachable moment.

How can you plan for the teachable moment?

I know that teachers must be prepared every day before they come to class, and although teachable moments might be ignored if a lesson plan is too strictly followed, teachers still do have to plan learning activities that are based on goals. That said, when I observe teachers in local schools using the types of instruction that high-stakes tests and new teacher evaluation models tend to spawn, I see teachable moments going unnoticed or ignored. And, I see students whose experience in school is narrowed to a set of skills and a base of knowledge they are neither excited about nor believe are important.

No, the teacher can't write a lesson plan for the teachable moment, but he or she can write a lesson plan that is flexible enough, so when the moment comes, the plan can include the new direction where the circumstances take the teacher and the students. Teachable moments might be the only ones in which children learn meaningful, sustainable, applicable, and relevant information and skills today. Their world is awash with information. Wikipedia, Alexa, Google, Siri, Twitter, and Facebook bombard them with information that trains them to look only for what matters to them right now. There is no shortage of information, fake or real, and prescriptive curricula like the Common Core and other state standards are irrelevant to them. But teachable moments have the potential to make academic learning pertinent, even in the 21st century.

The problem with academic standards is that they require the complex mapping of a whole school year's educational journey before even getting to know students. This fails to allow teachers to take their students on adventures. It's like going across country on a road trip without the flexibility to go off the beaten path, without having the freedom to explore unexpected events and to investigate unanticipated personal curiosities, where we will learn lessons we can apply across various aspects of our lives. The way our system forces us to teach, we must have a *map* that shows us very specifically where to go, including where we should stop, what we should do, and even prescribes exactly what we should learn in each place. Think of it like this: If our bus gets a flat tire near a mountain, our standardized system says there is no time to go for a hike to see the ancient Native American historical site nearby. We have to put the spare tire on quickly and get back on track. We must not let ourselves fall into any rabbit holes. We will miss the ancient pictographs carved in the rockface halfway up the mountain, but importantly, we won't miss the next common core standard, whatever it might be. Perhaps the next Common Core Standard is about ancient pictographs. Will our lesson on the origin of written linguistic signs hold meaning to our students, devoid of the context of their experience?

The *teachable moment* requires the kind of patience that policymakers do not have. It requires faith in teachers that department of education officials and some school administrators lack. It also requires letting go of a traditional curriculum that policymakers, school administrators, and academics are deeply invested in but that students are less invested in every day. It's not the content of these curricula that conflicts with the idea of the *teachable moment* as much as it is the structure and sequence of these curricula and the high level of control we placed on teachers to prescriptively teach specific information on specific days in specific ways. The best private schools in the world don't do this. Why should public schools?

What does a schoolteacher need to make use of teachable moments?

Teachers need to be brave and honest so they can go places where they do not know the answers any more than students do, so we can cast off our role as experts for that of a tour guide. We must be observant, patient, and present, so when the moment comes, we realize it and can seize the opportunity within it. We must understand how *to turn to* the moment, how to point at it, how to let go of our preconceived agendas and walk our students down an unexplored path, but also know when it's time to turn back. Sometimes the road is a dead end, but there is a lot of country out there, so we don't want to waste time looking for lessons at the dead end or making a narrowing path into a grand universe any more than we want to restrict the possibilities of what our students can learn because we must be in control of the time.

A Final Thought

When a teachable moment comes, don't ignore it; use it. It's a gift that no teacher ought to waste, but when Christmas is over, go back to work, thus inviting the next moment.

Don't worry. There will be a lesson in it.

· 1 5 ·

THE ROLE OF A TEACHER

When we make a career of teaching, it is important to revisit the question of what the role of a teacher is. This is nearly always a personal decision. Some of us develop our identification with a role because of our family, our own experience in school, and our mentors. As we evolve as teachers, we must reflect on the meaning of the work we do. Without meaning, teaching can be boring, absurd, tedious, and a grind. For us and for our students. But having even a loosely formed idea of what our role is can give teaching meaning. It can even become rewarding beyond imagination.

When I started out, I did not know what I thought about my role consciously, other than the vague notion that the teacher was an *expert in his or her subject area* and an *authority figure* in the classroom. But, because I was not an expert at ELA, not at 22 years old anyway, I did not feel like an authority. Instead, I *acted* like an authority, and my students sensed it, which made me feel like an imposter. I survived a few years teaching like this, but secretly, I felt like a fraud. I *was* a fraud and an imposter, because I wasn't clear about my purpose.

Not knowing my purpose or my role prevented me from forming the kind of bond with my students that I later, through my total failure as a teacher, learned was necessary for teaching and learning. My students couldn't trust me because I was not being me. I was not being "me," because I did not know who I was. As a result, my students resisted being themselves. We were strangers, acting roles for one another, a dynamic for which I take sole responsibility. Reflecting on our roles as teachers helps to prevent and solve this problem. Without role identification, there was no trust between me and my students. How could they ask me for help with their writing if they didn't trust me? How could they admit they didn't know something—simply ask a question about something they did not understand—if there was no relationship? I didn't know any of this was important at the time. I didn't know how pretentious I was being because I didn't know who I was. My students would have forgiven this since they did not know who they were yet either, but I was not only acting as if I were an expert, but I was acting as if I was sure of myself, too. I pretended that I was *more* than they were. I thought that students were different from teachers, that they were apart, separate, and other. This kind of thinking prevented me from building even a small sense of community in my classroom, which eventually failure and intuition goaded me into facing. Unfortunately, my head overruled my heart in those early days, and I kept on acting a role for which I was never cast.

I survived my first three years of teaching—despite my lack of intentional work on community building—because of three things: One. I had tremendous support from my bosses. Two. The skills-based curriculum was very clear and very practical. Three. I accidentally did show who I was to those students due to the fact that my first job was at a boarding school, where the classes were very small, faculty worked in the dorms at night and on weekends, and we ate meals with our students daily. We were together, it seemed, all the time. After days, weeks, months, and years, my identity seeped out around the edges of my mask. I couldn't pretend to be an expert all the time. Because we all lived with our students at that school, community was impossible to avoid. It was baked in, and I didn't know it.

The teacher's role can be that of the expert, but only if the person teaching is actually an expert. On the other hand, the teacher's role could be something else. Experts have a lot to offer, but they also possess internal (personality) barriers and external (social) barriers that often prevent them from being accessible to their students.

My next teaching job was in a public school, and things got really bad for me. Classroom management became a major problem. My students didn't buy the expert act at all. Even if I had been an expert at ELA, they didn't care one bit. Often, many of them didn't listen to me when I talked. Some even talked over me. They baited me into confrontations. They often did not complete or even start their classwork. The few students who were interested in learning something in my classes were disgusted with me because I could not control the class. My attempts to punish bad behavior were completely ineffective.

I dreaded going to work, feeling like a fraud. Unproductive and disconnected, I was forced to face the fact that I was a bad teacher. By then, I had a master's degree in English and could legitimately call myself an expert, but I felt like a failure. By the end of my first year at that school, I needed to change my teaching or quit. I decided that I would quit my job—maybe quit teaching altogether—because I didn't know how or what to change in order to get it right. I was in a desperate place, which, although I didn't know it then, was an unexpected and powerful gift that would change me forever. There is something about desperation that makes the right choices crystal clear, no matter how terrified we are of them.

During the summer that followed that bad year when I planned to quit, I don't know why exactly, but I procrastinated. For some reason, resigning was not something that came easily. Before I knew it, the last week of August had come around. With only a few days before the first day of the school year, I decided I would go back. I am ashamed to admit that my plan for that year was not about improving my teaching, changing my methods, getting help, and definitely not about becoming the good teacher I eventually became. Not at all. I did not have the confidence to even consider that I could improve at that point. Instead, I planned to go back for another year and loaf around until my bosses caught me doing nothing and fired me. There were a few cynical, burnt-out teachers who I figured I could hang out with while waiting for someone to notice I was not doing anything. This was a shamefully unprofessional and irresponsible plan, but I was in a dark place, and I didn't know how to get out of it. Strangely and totally by accident, I learned that the only way out is through.

Because I started my school year doing nothing, I stopped working, stopped trying, and stopped trying to be someone I wasn't. Even if I were an expert, I didn't have it in me to act that way anymore. I still can't. I guess I am not that kind of person. The pain of my failure as a teacher forced me to explore who I had become, who I was, and eventually who I wanted to be. I had thought I might be a defender of weak and vulnerable children, because I had been bullied in school when I was a child. But, no. That wasn't me. I had to let that go. It hurt to know that I could not prevent the pervasive meanness that was all around me, but punishing perpetrators only became an opportunity for displaced and unresolved rage for people from my past. I was becoming the perpetrator, whom I hated so much. I was certainly not an expert. I was not much of a warrior teacher. My old wounds were too deep and unexplored back then to be useful to me, and they became what Carl Jung defined as "the shadow self," defining me subconsciously and robbing me and my students of the joy that teaching and learning not only can be but must be, stealing from us the possibility of how wonderful our relationship could be.

The role I would eventually embody as a teacher became impossible to ignore the more I let go of being who I was not and owned who I was. This was difficult at first because my teacher identity did not match any conventional image of a teacher, and all I ever wanted to be growing up was normal. But I am not normal. Never have been. Never will be. Embracing the teacher who I discovered I am, though, made my job infinitely easier. To this day, I still identify myself in this way, partly because it requires so little effort but mostly because it is so me. My role became that of teacher as helper. I woke up one morning, put on my clothes, looked in the mirror, and told myself *it was time to help kids learn to read and write.* The pressure was off. I didn't need to prove anything. I didn't have to do much either. All there was left to do was be me. And that was easier than I had imagined. Once I stopped trying to be someone or something else and once I stopped trying to do things that I assumed were the correct things teachers do, I was able to trust myself, and my students were able to trust me Wu Wei.

This was transformative. I showed up one day, and my students sensed the change immediately. I felt like they saw me. They did, because I was there when I had not been before. I had been using coercion, incentives, rewards, and force in my teaching, but then I began to see them, listen to them, care about them, and accept them for who they were instead. I accepted that they did not like the books I liked and that they did not want to be in school. The curriculum I had thought must get done—material that I thought I should "cover"—took a back seat to our relationship and to my curiosity about them.

I learned that it's never too late to find out who you are and to be that person.

The first day of school that year, when I decided to loaf around doing nothing, I was immediately bored and restless. Although I had stopped teaching in any conventional way and decided to be unprofessional, ironically, I began teaching for the very first time. I did not use the books that the other English teachers were using. Back then, they thought of their curriculum in terms of the titles of books. "I'm teaching *Catcher in the Rye* this month," a teacher might say. I did not assign homework. I did not give quizzes or tests. I de-emphasized grades to the point where they were barely relevant.

My bosses didn't even notice this change at first. The only thing that got their attention was that I had stopped sending students to the office for bad behavior. I didn't stop teaching. I just took a lot of time to get to know my students, and I spent our time helping my students with their reading and writing, especially their writing, which was pretty bad. I also helped them be nicer to one another. They just hadn't learned how. Nobody had taught them how to be fair and polite, to be sensitive to other people's feelings, and to take responsibility for their own mistakes. So, instead of punishing them for "getting out of line," I assisted them in understanding what they were doing and helped them see the consequences of their actions and the precursors to those moments when they were mean or disrespectful.

It was not a clean process for me or them. It was not organized, and the results varied and sometimes were so severely delayed that I could not see the return on my investments, which was frustrating at first. I was experimenting and not fully aware of what I was doing, where we were going, and what my goal was, except that I had to keep it real. I knew when it was real because I could feel it. I felt alive as a teacher for the first time, and alive as a person for the first time in a long while.

By understanding that my purpose in their lives was to *help* them, not to be an expert or an authority—not to force them to do anything or fear me if they didn't comply—they began to understand what they were reading, began questioning the ideas they saw in texts, and expressed those thoughts in words both spoken and written for the first time. They even stopped interrupting me and one another. They started asking for help.

Knowing the special role that you will play in the lives of your students will partially be intentional, meaning you will decide to identify with the role. And it will partially be automatic, meaning you will only need to be yourself. This will require significant personal reflection. You will try on many hats and feel both deep pain when you wear the wrong hat and absolute joy when you find the one that was made for you. It will absolutely require as much patience as you can muster to sit with yourself in this process. You don't have to be absolutely sure what your role is, but you need to work on it, or else the daily work of the job will lack meaning, focus, and direction. Your idea of what teaching is and who you are as a teacher will become your compass. This idea will guide you in your decision-making for choices big and small. Others will want us to enact a different role, but once we have embodied our chosen role, the one that fits us, it will be easy to defend our purpose.

Whether you are trying to decide what to do tomorrow with your students, what message to communicate in the feedback you give them on their work, or how much or what kind of work to give them, the organizing principles that guide your decisions must coalesce around your idea of who you are as a teacher. Since most of us attended school for many years ourselves, we incorporate our understanding of what a teacher's role is without being conscious of it. Some of us think that since we turned out alright, the methods that our teachers used were fine. But our students might not be like us. Maybe they learn differently. Mine did. Also, maybe we didn't learn all we could. Shouldn't we do better than our teachers did, if we can?

Some of us were very lucky and had fantastic teachers, but that begs the question. What makes a good teacher? What do good teachers do? Are they performers? Coaches? Taskmasters? Disciplinarians? Experts in their content areas? Do they need to be warm and caring? Or, should they be tough and detached? Some people believe that the best teachers wear different hats depending on who their students are. One student may need a drill sergeant, while another needs a counselor.

Sometimes the best way to think about your role as a teacher is through a metaphor.

A teacher could see his or her role as a banker, where his or her primary action is depositing information into students' heads. Now, that would not be the metaphor that I would subscribe to. Paulo Freire wouldn't like that much either, but you might. That metaphor would require the person to see the teacher as an expert, a possessor of knowledge as truth, and the controller of the answers. The person would have to envision students as empty, ignorant, compliant, and passive—willing to learn.

Before I rejected that role, I acted as if I were a banker, daily trying to deposit information into my students' heads, a perspective that governed all my actions. It informed me of all my plans, oriented my curriculum, and guided my responses to students' behavior, both academic and social. Even my posture was affected. The classroom was a place I tried to control and maintain control over. I saw my students as needing external knowledge rather than internal knowledge, external motivation, rather than internal motivation, external approval instead of internal acceptance. I believed that their perspectives had to match mine. Otherwise, they were wrong. That perspective required me to place the curriculum at the center of my teaching, as opposed to seeing relationships as most important.

I learned the hard way that I had been wrong about teaching, wrong about my students, wrong about curriculum, and most disastrously, wrong about me, so I was hesitant to adopt a new approach. Thank God. Instead, I was open to new ideas and new paradigms. Being wrong is a fantastic learning experience, which is how I learned to become a very good teacher. Being wrong is painful, which motivates us. I know the pain I felt from my failure got me off my ass.

I considered that perhaps my role as teacher was more of a gardener. Would I plant seeds, be patient, observe more, and do less? Would I create the conditions for growth instead of trying to force it to happen? My students would be allowed to become what they are rather than have academic content imposed on them, like the many standards for learning that the government requires teachers to teach. As a gardener, the curriculum would be less important than individual students. Maybe that was me.

Or, maybe I was a chef? This metaphor promoted the idea that, as a teacher, I would construct learning activities that were nourishing and palatable. There would be as much art as science when teaching is like cooking. The students' fulfillment and, ultimately, their experience would matter. Perhaps I was a chef, I considered. Or. Was I a trainer? I could focus mostly on skills, repetition, and mastery. I would take a special, individual, and diagnostic approach to each student's performance. Progress would be as important as results. That might be me, I thought.

Was I more of a coach? I would promote a team approach, facilitate more than lecture, and model more than direct. I would understand the game, know my players, and know their strengths and weaknesses. Strategy would be important. Sometimes the heart would matter, sometimes the head. That could have been my metaphor for teaching.

As I tried on these different teacher identities, I also considered that I might be like a carpenter. Like the chef, I would have an orientation toward methods of construction, toward learning as experience, and would be less involved with experimentation than the scientist or the artist might be. As a carpenter-teacher, I would balance physicality with pragmatism. Craft would be important, as would engineering. Structural integrity and utility would be offset by architecture and aesthetics. So many of these roles had something to offer.

I considered the role of the teacher as an artist, which suggested that there are no right ways, only beautiful ones. I would be highly experimental, blending convention with innovation. Both rejecting tradition and embracing it at the same time, I would be concerned with mastery, representation, and using my special knowledge in various mediums and practicing different techniques. The artist is concerned with subjectivity more than objectivity, and I felt as if I might be getting closer to a role that could be mine.

But then I considered the role of the scientist. Even more concerned with experimentation, I would use trial and error with my students, maintaining a high tolerance for error and failure, like artists and entrepreneurs. Learning could be as much about how processes do not work as how processes do work. My attention might as much on success or achievement as authentic understandings. Serendipity and epiphany would become important to honor. Could I be the artist *and* the scientist, I wondered?

I also considered that perhaps the philosopher would be a good paradigm to emulate as a teacher. I would be Socratic, asking questions more than answering them. Discussion, dialog, and inquiry would be my means, and exploration of meaning would be my primary concern. Maybe if I were a librarian-style teacher, I would offer a myriad of resources; learning would be about the educational environment, the decor, the availability of information, and access. I would be an assistant more than an assessor.

I tried on the hat of the storyteller teacher, using the power of narrative to transform, transmit, and relate information, experience, and understanding. Using stories also transferred that creative power to my students, fostering their creativity and their ability to synthesize information and ideas. It gave them freedom through language and power through voice. I was convinced for a long time that I was a narrative teacher. I still think I am sometimes. There are so many more metaphors that can be used as lenses through which to see which role you want to identify with as you teach. And the point is not to adopt any one metaphor. It is to think through which one best describes your teaching style, so you can become yourself. This will help you understand your own beliefs about how people learn, so you can own your philosophical ground or change it. You will likely adopt more than one such paradigm, but you will just as likely be able to identify one that you do not agree with. Sometimes you will have many of these roles at once, and over the years you will likely change hats many times as you learn who you are and what works with your students.

Do you see teaching as the work of a machine? Then you are an engineer. Maybe you see instruction as both diagnostic and therapeutic. Then, teaching follows the medical model for you. Doctor as teacher? Perhaps your ethic is one of care, so you see being a teacher as something like nursing, counseling, or social work. If you think children need surveillance, maybe you are like a prison guard or police officer. If you are trying to convince your students to assimilate new knowledge, then you might see teaching as sales or maybe as litigation. I have seen all of these styles in my career as an educator, but often those I observe are unaware of their identity as a teacher and even unaware of the concept. And, in my work as a university professor of education and an education consultant, I observe many teachers who do not know what lens they look through when they work with their students.

When a teacher does understand that he or she sees himself or herself as the warrior-as-teacher, the monk-as-teacher, the performer-as-teacher, or something else, he or she is so effective that they seem magical to anyone who watches them. When teachers are conscious of how they conceive their role and their teacher identity, they become present in a whole new way.

Eventually, I became quite good at classroom management because I managed my students' behavior less and taught them about emotional regulation more. But it helped that I had a clue what my role was. I have consistently identified with any role that was a *helper*. Some days I was like a doctor or nurse; I helped them heal and cared for them. Other days, I was like a lawyer, defending them from others or even themselves. I was like a coach or trainer, conditioning them and leading them to perform better. Like a librarian, I showed them the resources they could use. Like a priest or rabbi, I nourished their spirits. Sometimes I was like a counselor, acknowledging their pain. And other times, I was tougher on my students, challenging them to meet up with their better selves.

No matter what role I embodied, I found it easiest and most natural to frame my teaching as *helping*, and I still do. I still get stuck sometimes, not knowing whether to do this or that, but all I have to do when that happens is ask myself, What can I do that will help my students? And then, I know the answer. Now, that's just me. You may be different. As Parker Palmer says in his book *The Courage to Teach*, "Technique is what teachers use until the real teacher arrives." I wasn't a real teacher until I let go of what I thought I should be and embraced who I was and who I was becoming. If we are not real with our students, they won't show us who they are, and then helping them is impossible. That's who I am—as a teacher. Who are you?

REFERENCES

Abuhamdeh, S., & Csikszentmihalyi, M. (2012). Attentional involvement and intrinsic motivation. *Motivation and Emotion, 36*, 257–267.
Allen, J. P., Kuperminc, G., Philliber, S., & Herre, K. (1994). Programmatic prevention of adolescent problem behaviors: The role of autonomy, relatedness, and volunteer service in the Teen Outreach Program. *American Journal of Community Psychology, 22*(5), 595–615.
Anderman, L. H., & Midgley, C. (1998). Motivation and middle school students. perspective, 26(3/4), 325-346.
Bakhtin, M. M. (1981). *The dialogic imagination: Four essays*. M. Holquist (Ed). C. Emerson & M. Holquist. Trans. University of Texas Press.
Bakhtin, M. M. (2010). *Speech genres and other late essays*. University of Texas Press.
Bandura, A. (1986). *Social foundations of thought and action*.
Bandura, A. (1999 & 1977). *Self-efficacy: The exercise of control*.
Bandura, A., & Walters, R. H. (1963). *Social learning and personality development*.
Bible, K. J. (1996). *King James Bible* (Vol. 19). Proquest.
Blackburn, B. R. (2013a). *Rigor made easy: Getting started*. Routledge.
Blackburn, B. R. (2013b). *Rigor is not a four-letter word*. Eye on education.
Blackburn, B. R. (2017). *Rigor and assessment in the classroom*. Taylor & Francis.
Bloom, B. S. (1956). *Taxonomy of educational objectives: The classification of educational goals*.
Brandenburg, W. E. (1905). *Philosophic basis for the beginning of Christianity*. Drake University.
Brophy, J. E., & Good, T. L. (1974). *Teacher-student relationships: Causes and consequences*. Holt, Rinehart & Winston.

Brown, B. (2015). *Daring greatly: How the courage to be vulnerable transforms the way we live, love, parent, and lead.* Penguin.

Brown, J., & Langer, E. (1990). Mindfulness and intelligence: A comparison. Educational psychologist, 25(3-4), 305-335.

Brown, S. L. (2009). *Play: How it shapes the brain, opens the imagination, and invigorates the soul.* Penguin.

Bruner, J. (1973). *The relevance of education* (No. 690). WW Norton & Company.

Bruner, J. (1979). On knowing: Essays for the left hand. Cambridge, MA: Belknap Press.

Bruner, J. (2020). *The culture of education.* Harvard University Press.

Bruner, J., & Haste, H. (Eds.). (2010). Making sense *(Routledge revivals): The child's construction of the world.* Routledge.

Christenson, S. L., Reschly, A. L., & Wylie, C. (Eds.). (2012). *Handbook of research on student engagement.* Springer Science & Business Media.

Coffman, C., & Sorensen, K. (2013). *Culture eats strategy for lunch: The secret of extraordinary results, igniting the passion within.* Modern Press.

Coles, R. (1989). *The call of stories: Teaching and the moral imagination.* Houghton Mifflin Harcourt.

Cook, C. R., Fiat, A., Larson, M., Daikos, C., Slemrod, T., Holland, E. A., Thayer, A., & Renshaw, T. (2018). Positive greetings at the door: Evaluation of a low-cost, high-yield proactive classroom management strategy. *Journal of Positive Behavior Interventions, 20*(3), 149–159.

Cordova, D., & Lepper, M. R. (1996). Intrinsic motivation and the process of learning: Beneficial effects of contextualization, personalization, and choice. *Journal of Educational Psychology,* 88(4):715–730.

Csikszentmihalyi, M. (1975). *Beyond boredom and anxiety: Experiencing flow in work and play.* Jossey-Bass.

Csikszentmihalyi, M (1990). *Flow: The psychology of optimal experience.* Harper and Row.

Csikszentmihalyi, M. (1997). *Flow and education. NAMTA Journal, 22*(2), 2–35.

Csikszentmihalyi, M. (2014). *Applications of flow in human development and education.* Springer

Deci, E. L. (1975). *Intrinsic motivation.* Plenum.

Deci, E. L., & Flaste, R. (1995). *Why we do what we do: The dynamics of personal autonomy.* GP Putnam's Sons.

Deci, E. L., & Ryan, R. M. (1985). *Intrinsic motivation and self-determination in human behavior.* Plenum.

Deci, E. L. & Ryan, R. M. (1987). The support of autonomy and control of behavior. *Journal of Personality and Social Psychology, 53*(6), 1024–1037.

Dewey, J. (1897). *My pedagogic creed* (No. 25). EL Kellogg & Company.

Dewey, J. (1916). *Democracy and education.*

Dewey, J. (1986). Experience and education. In *The educational forum* (Vol. 50, No. 3, pp. 241–252). Taylor & Francis Group.

Docan, T. N. (2006). Positive and negative incentives in the classroom: An analysis of grading systems and student motivation. *Journal of Scholarship of Teaching and Learning, 6*(2), 21–40.

Duckworth, A. (2016). *Grit: The power of passion and perseverance.* Scribner.

Dweck, C. S. (1986). Motivational processes affecting learning. *American Psychologist*, 41(10), 1040–1048.

Dweck, C. S. (2008). *Mindset: The new psychology of success*. Random House.

Dweck, C.S. (2010). Even geniuses work hard. *Educational Leadership*, 68(1), 16–20.

Dweck, C. S. (2013). *Self-theories: Their role in motivation, personality, and development*. Psychology Press.

Dweck, C. S., & Master, A. (2009). Self-theories and motivation. *Handbook of motivation at school*, 123.

Finn, J. D. (1989). Withdrawing from school. *Review of Educational Research*, 59(2), 117–142.

Finn, J. D. (1993). *School engagement and students at risk*. National Center for Education Statistics.

Finn, J. D., & Rock, D. A. (1997). Academic success among students at risk for school failure. *Journal of Applied Psychology*, 82, 221–234.

Eklund, K., O'Malley, M., & Meyer, L. (2017). Gauging mindfulness in children and youth: School - based applications. *Psychology in the Schools*, 54(1), 101–114.

Epstein, M. (2014). *The trauma of everyday life*. Penguin.

Lawson, P. J., & Flocke, S. A. (2009). Teachable moments for health behavior change: a concept analysis. *Patient education and counseling*, 76(1), 25-30.

Fredricks, J. A., Blumenfeld, P. C., & Paris, A. H. (2004). School engagement: Potential of the concept, state of the evidence. *Review of Educational Research*, 74(1), 59–109.

Freire, P. (1996). *Pedagogy of the oppressed*. Continuum.

Freire, P., & Ara, A. M. (1998). *Pedagogy of the heart*. Bloomsbury Publishing USA.

Gable, R. A., Hester, P. H., Rock, M. L., & Hughes, K. G. (2009). Back to basics: Rules, praise, ignoring, and reprimands revisited. *Intervention in School and Clinic*, 44(4) 195–205.

Gardner, H. (1993). *Frames of mind: The theory of multiple intelligences* (10 anniversary ed.). Basic Books.

Geers, A. L., Weiland, P. E., Kosbab, K., Landry, S. J., & Helfer, S. G. (2005). Goal activation, expectations, and the placebo effect. *Journal of Personality and Social Psychology*, 89(2), 143–159.

Ghasemi, S. H., Adel, S. M. R., & Zareian, G. (2015). The analysis of authoritative and persuasive discourse of Iranian EFL teachers and their roles at public and private schools. *International Journal of Education and Research*, 3(2), 91–104.

Gibbs, B. (2017). Rigor for What? Social studies teacher conceptions and enactments of instructional rigor. *The Social Studies*, 108(5), 192–203.

Gibbs, B. (2021). How to define and apply rigor. *Principal leadership*. National Association of Secondary School Principals (NASSP).

Ginott, H. G. (1965). *Between parent and child: New solutions to old problems*.

Goleman, D. (1996). Emotional intelligence. Why it can matter more than IQ. *Learning*, 24(6), 49–50.

Goleman, D. (2020). *Emotional intelligence*. Bloomsbury Publishing.

Goodman, J. F. (2013). Charter management organizations and the regulated environment: Is it worth the price? *Educational Researcher* 42(2), 89–96.

Greenberg, M. T. (2023). *Evidence for social and emotional learning in schools*. Learning Policy Institute.

Greene, B. A. (2015). Measuring cognitive engagement with self-report scales: Reflections from over 20 years of research. *Educational Psychologists, 50*(1), 14–30.

Grolnick, W. S., & Ryan, R. M. (1987). Autonomy in children's learning: An experimental and individual difference investigation. *Journal of Personality and Social Psychology, 52*, 890–898.

Grolnick, W. S., Ryan, R. M., & Deci, E. L. (1991). Inner resources for school achievement: Motivational mediators of children's perceptions of their parents. *Journal of Educational Psychology, 83*(4), 508.

Havighurst, R. J. (1953). *Human development and education*. Longmans.

Hayek, F. (1980). *Individualism and economic order*. University of Chicago Press.

Hechinger Institute. (2009). *Understanding and reporting on academic rigor*. Retrieved from http://hechinger.tc.columbia.edu/primers/Hechinger Institute_Rigor_Primer.pdf (August 2, 2020).

Herodotus (2015) [c. 430 BC]. Tomvs alter: Libri V-IX continens. In N. G. Wilson (Ed.). *Herodoti Historiae*. Oxford University Press.

Hogarth, R. M. (2001). *Educating intuition*. University of Chicago Press.

Hollis, S. (2014). *Cognitive effects and academic consequences of video game playing*.

Hollis, S. (2016). *Brain drain or brain gain? Cognitive skill training with novice video game players with casual video games*.

James, W. (1983, 1899). *Talks to teachers on psychology and to students on some of life's ideals*. Harvard University Press.

Jenkins, J. R., & Deno, S. L. (1969). Influence of student behavior on teacher's self-evaluation. *Journal of Educational Psychology, 60*(6p1), 439.

Kaplan, A. (2017). *The conduct of inquiry: Methodology for behavioural Science*. Routledge.

King Jr, M. L. (1963). *Letter from Birmingham jail*.

Kirsch, I. (1985). Response expectancy as a determinant of experience and behavior. *American Psychologist, 40*(11), 1189–1202.

Kish, D. (2009). Human echolocation: How to "see" like a bat. *New Scientist, 202*(2703), 31–33.

Klem, A. M., & Connell, J. P. (2004). Relationships matter: Linking teacher support to student engagement and achievement. *Journal of School Health, 74*(4), 1–47.

Kohn, A. (1992). *No contest: The case against competition*. Houghton Mifflin Harcourt.

Kolb, D. A. (2014). *Experiential learning: Experience as the source of learning and development*. FT Press.

Lahey, J. (2015). *The gift of failure: How to step back and let your child succeed*. Hachette UK.

Lao Tzu, L. E. (1997). *Tao te ching*. Wordsworth.

Langer, E. J. (1989). *Mindfulness*. Addison-Wesley/Addison Wesley Longman.

Langer, E. J. (1993). A mindful education. *Educational Psychologist, 28*(1), 43–50.

Langer, E. J. (2016). *The power of mindful learning*. Hachette UK.

Lefcourt, H. M. (1991). *Locus of control*. Academic Press.

REFERENCES

Lepper, M. R. & Greene, D. (1975). Turning play into work: Effects of adult surveillance and extrinsic rewards on children's intrinsic motivation. *Journal of Personality and Social Psychology, 31*(3), 479–486.

Lepper, M. R., & Greene, D. (2015). *The hidden costs of reward: New perspectives on the psychology of human motivation.* Psychology Press.

Maslow, A. (1943). A theory of human motivation. *Psychological Review, 50*(4), 370–396.

Maslow, A. (1954, 1987). *Motivation and personality.*

Maslow, A. (1966). *The psychology of science: A reconnaissance.* Gateway Editions.

Maslow, A. (1971). *The farther reaches of human nature* (Vol. 19711). Viking Press.

Maslow, A. (1974). *A theory of human motivation.*

Maslow, A. (2013). *Toward a psychology of being.* Simon and Schuster.

McClelland, D. C. (1987). *Human motivation.* University of Cambridge.

McClelland, D. C., Atkinson, J. W., Clark, R. A., & Lowell, E. L. (1953). *The achievement motive.* Appleton-Century-Crofts.

Montessori, M. (1959). *The absorbent mind.*

Mutch, C. (2021). Maslow before bloom: Implementing a caring pedagogy during Covid-19. *Teachers' Work, 18*(2), 69–90.

Newmann, F. M., Marks, H. M., & Gamoran, A. (1996). Authentic pedagogy and student performance. *American Journal of Education, 104*(4), 280–312.

Nietzsche, F. (1886). *Beyond good & evil: Prelude to a philosophy of the future.* Vintage.

Noddings, N. (1988). An ethic of caring and its implications for instructional arrangements. *American Journal of Education, 96*(2), 215–230.

Noddings, N. (2013). *Caring: A relational approach to ethics and moral education.* University of California Press.

Noddings, N. (2015). *The challenge to care in schools* (2nd ed.). Teachers College Press.

Noddings, N. (2018). *Philosophy of education.* Routledge.

Palmer, P. J. (2017). *The courage to teach: Exploring the inner landscape of a teacher's life.* John Wiley & Sons.

Pellegrino, J. W. & Hilton, M. L. (2012). *Education for life and work: Developing transferable knowledge and skills in the 21st century.* National Academies Press.

Pert, C. B. (2010). *Molecules of emotion: The science behind mind-body medicine.* Simon and Schuster.

Pink, D. H. (2011). *Drive: The surprising truth about what motivates us.* Penguin.

Pokhrel, S., & Chhetri, R. (2021). A literature review on impact of Covid-19 pandemic on teaching and learning. *Higher Education for the Future, 8*(1), 133–141.

Poll, G. S. (2015). *Engaged today—ready for tomorrow.* US Overall Fall.

Pollard, R. (2018). *Dialogue and desire: Mikhail Bakhtin and the linguistic turn in psychotherapy.* Routledge.

Reeve, J. (2001). *Understanding motivation and human emotion* (3rd ed.). Harcourt.

Reeve, J. (2002). Self-determination theory applied to educational settings. In E. L. Deci & R. M. Ryan (Eds.), *Handbook of self-determination research* (pp. 183–203). University of Rochester Press.

Reeve, J., Jang, H., Carrell, D., Jeon, S., & Barch, J. (2004). Enhancing students' engagement by increasing teachers' autonomy support. *Motivation and Emotion, 28*(2), 147–169.

Renshaw, T. L., & Cook, C. R. (2017). Introduction to the special issue: Mindfulness in the schools—Historical roots, current status, and future directions. *Psychology in the Schools, 54*(1), 5–12.

Reyes, M., Brackett, M., Rivers, S, White, M., and Peter Salovey. (2012). Classroom emotional climate, student engagement, and academic achievement. *Journal of Educational Psychology, 104*(3), 700–712.

Rosenthal, R., & Jacobson, L. (1968a). Pygmalion in the classroom. *The Urban Review, 3*(1), 16–20.

Rosenthal, R., & Jacobson, L. (1968b). *Pygmalion in the classroom: Teacher expectation and pupils' intellectual development*. Holt, Rinehart & Winston.

Rotter, J. B. (1966). Generalized expectancies for internal versus external control of reinforcement. *Psychological Monographs: General and Applied, 80*(1), 1.

Ruiz, M. (2011). *The four agreements: A practical guide to personal freedom*. Amber-Allen Publishing.

Ryan, R. M., & Deci, E. L. (2007). Active human nature: Self-determination theory and the promotion and maintenance of sport, exercise, and health. *Intrinsic Motivation and Self-Determination in Exercise and Sport*, 1–19.

Ryan, R. M. & Deci, E. L. (2017). *Self-determination theory: Basic psychological needs in motivation, development, and wellness*. The Guilford Press, a division of Guilford Publications, Inc.

Ryan, R. M., & Grolnick, W. S. (1986). Origins and pawns in the classroom: Self-report and projective assessments of individual differences in children's perceptions. *Journal of Personality and Social Psychology, 50*(3), 550–558.

Savoie, J. M. & Hughes, A. (1994). Problem-based learning as classroom solution. *Educational Leadership, 52*(3), 54–57.

Seifert, T. (2004). Understanding student motivation. *Educational Research, 46*(2), 137–149.

Shor, I., & Freire, P. (1987). *A pedagogy for liberation: Dialogues and transforming education*. Greenwood Publishing Group.

Slingerland, E. (2015). *Trying not to try: Art and science of spontaneity*. Crown.

Spielberger, C. (2004). *Encyclopedia of applied psychology*. Academic Press.

Sullivan, C. (2003). *The benefits of parent-child play for the social development of preschoolers with varying levels of anxiety problems* (Doctoral dissertation, Concordia University).

Thorndike, L., & Bruce, D. (2017). *Animal intelligence: Experimental studies*. Routledge.

Tomlinson, C. A., & Doubet, K. (2005). Reach them to teach them. *Educational Leadership, 62*(7), 8–15.

Tyler, R. W. (2010, 1949). *Basic principles of curriculum and instruction*. University of Chicago Press.

Van der Kolk, B. (2014). *The body keeps the score: Brain, mind, and body in the healing of trauma*. Penguin.

Vygotsky, L. S. (1980). *Mind in society: The development of higher psychological processes*. Harvard University Press.

Washor, E., & Mojkowski, C. (2007). What do you mean by rigor? *Education Leadership*, 64, 84–87.

Wesley, J. (1831). *Sermons on several occasions* (Vol. 1). J. Emory and B. Waugh.

Wiggins, G. P., & McTighe, J. (2005). *Understanding by design*. ASCD.

Williams, W. C. (1984). The use of force. In *The doctor stories* (pp. 56–60).

Williams, W. C. (1992). *Paterson* (Vol. 806). New Directions Publishing.

Zenner, C., Herrnleben-Kurz, S., & Walach, H. (2014). Mindfulness-based interventions in schools—a systematic review and meta-analysis. *Frontiers in Psychology*, 5, 603.

Zyngier, D. (2008). (Re)conceptualizing student engagement: Doing education not doing time. *Teaching and Teacher Education*, 24(7), 1765–1776.

INDEX

A

3M 78
The absorbent mind (book) 132
Abuhamdeh, Sami 40
academic achievement 14
academic learning 8, 39, 67, 96, 136
academic outcomes 14, 19, 36, 46, 74, 121, 128
academic rigor 91–8
academic subjects 18
addiction 19, 28, 73
attention deficit hyperactivity disorder (ADHD) 73
adrenaline 100–2
affective domain 13, 19
Alexander the Great 123
American Psychological Association (APA) 87
amygdala 22, 69, 87, 99–103
amygdala hijacking 69, 99, 102–3
Apple, Michael 59

Aristotle 123
assimilation 56, 59–60

B

backward design 66
Bakhtin, Mikhail 32, 36, 48–9, 56, 116
Bandura, Albert 21, 29, 40, 55–6, 88, 115–16
Basic Principles of Curriculum and Instruction (book) 66–7
Batman 109–10
Beatles 79
Behaviorism 28, 30–2
being-cognition (B-Cognition) 32, 38
belief-behave-influence pattern 108–9
best practices 10, 46, 123
Beyond Good and Evil: Prelude to a Philosophy of the Future (book) 46
Blackburn, Barbara 93, 95
Bloom, Benjamin 18–20
Bloom, Harold 94

Bloom's Taxonomy 18–20, 22–3, 93–4
Brady, Tom 16
Brandenburg, Walter 131
Brooklyn College 16
Brophy, Jere 28
Brown, Stewart 98
Bruner, Jerome 29, 40, 47, 110
B-values 32–3

C

The Call of stories: Teaching and the moral imagination (book) 85
Caring: A Feminist Approach to Ethics and Moral Education (book) 33
Catcher in the Rye (book) 142
Chapman University 59
classical conditioning 26, 31
classroom management 30–1, 140, 147
cognitive domain 19
cognitive function 28, 125
Coles, Robert 85
Columbia University 16
communitas 65, 120
compliance-based model 10, 43–50
The Conduct of inquiry: Methodology for Behavioral Science (book) 31
confirmation bias 31
Confucius 57
constructivist (constructivism) 26, 56, 121
content literacy 7
Cook, Clayton 120
Copeland, Misty 16
Cortisol 100–2
The Courage to Teach (book) 71, 147
critical pedagogy 58–9
Csikszentmihalyi, Mihaly 38–40, 98
The culture of education 110
Cunningham, Robert 48, 65, 103
curriculum
 assessment-centered 56
 hidden 53
 outcomes-based 56, 67, 129
 skills-based 56, 140
 standards-based 19, 54, 56, 67, 121
 student-centered 40, 55, 57

D

d-cognition 32
Deci, Edward 35, 37, 39
deep learning 26, 28, 64
deficiency needs 17, 19–20
Democracy 59
Deno, Stanley 112
depression 14, 73, 83
developmental trauma 86
Dewey, John 40, 55, 57–8, 72, 134
dialogue 36, 53, 57, 94–5
differentiation 33, 92
diphtheria 83–5
disequilibration 57
District Determined Measures (DDM) 98
Doubet, Kristina 40
drug abuse 14
dualism 8, 122, 129
Duckworth, Angela 108
Dweck, Carol 28, 108, 112–14

E

educational objective (see *instructional objective*) 18–19, 66
Elementary and Secondary Education Act of 1965 55, 66
Emerson, Ralph-Waldo 57
emotional distress 14
Emotional Intelligence 31, 97, 125
Emotional Intelligence (book) 100
emotional safety 96, 105
Encyclopedia of applied psychology (book) 37
epinephrine 102
Epstein, Mark 3
Erikson, Erik 29
ethic of care 13, 16, 33, 46, 70, 74, 121

INDEX

executive functioning 86
expectancy theory 27–8
expectation messaging 116
experiential learning 40, 121, 134
external locus of control 113
extinction 29

F

The FAR Cycle (Formative Assessment for Results) 98
Farther reaches of human nature (book) 31–2, 50
fight or flight response 100–1
fixed mindset 112–13
flow theory 27, 39
Formative Assessment for Results (book) 98
The Four Agreements (book) 44, 121
Freire, Paulo 29, 40, 58, 95, 144
frontal cortices 87, 99–100
Fry, Arthur 78
F-Values 33

G

Gibbs, Brian 94
The Gift of Failure (book) 125
Ginott, Hiam 6
Giroux, Henry 53, 59
global pandemic 96–7
Goleman, Daniel 87, 100–1
Google 78–9, 136
gravity of being 63–72
the great mistake 28, 31, 50
Grolnick, Wendy 36
growth mindset 28, 112–14
growth needs 20–1

H

Havighurst, Robert 133

Hayek, Friedrich 57
hidden pedagogy 52–3
hierarchy of needs 17–18, 20–2, 55
high-stakes testing 19, 46, 81, 128–9
Hippocratic Oath 90
Hirsch, E.D. 94
Hogarth, Robin 28
Holt, John 59
Homer 123
Human development and education (book) 134
humanism 32
humanist pedagogy 55

I

instructional methodologies 60
instructional objective (see *educational objective*) 66
internally persuasive discourse 32, 116
interpersonal relationship 40
intuition 4, 11, 28, 69, 140
IQ (cognitive intelligence quotient) 111–12

J

Jackson, Philip 53
Jacobson, Lenore 111–14
James, William 27, 66, 68–70, 84, 125
Jefferson, Thomas 57
Jenkins, Joseph 112
Jung, Carl 125, 142

K

Kant, Immanuel 57
Kaplan, Abraham 31
Kincholoe, Joe 59
King Philip of Macedonia 123
Kish, Daniel 109–10
Kolb, David 40, 134
Kozol, Johnathan 59

L

Lao Tzu 37
Langer, Ellen 36, 73–4, 79–81, 94–5, 98
law of effect 28–9, 54
law of the instrument 31
Lewin, Kurt 40, 134
liberal education 57–8
liberal pedagogies 56–7, 59
limbic system 99–100, 102
Locke, John 57
Locus of control 16, 28, 113

M

Maslow, Abraham 16–17, 22–3, 105
Maslow's hammer 25–33
McClelland, David 21–2
McLaren, Peter 59
McMaster University 59
McTighe, Jay 55–66
mental health 97
the mind-body problem 116
Mindfulness 73–81
Mindfulness (book) 36
mindlessness 79–81
Mindset: The new psychology of success (book) 108
Modeling 115, 120, 122, 128
Montessori, Maria 40, 132
motivation
  extrinsic 35–6
  intrinsic 21, 34–41, 69, 86, 123, 125, 127
Motivation and Personality (book) 105
Mutch, Carol 96

N

National Association of Secondary School Principals (NASSP) 94
National Institute for Play 98
narrative discourse 32

National Assessment for Educational Progress (NAEP) 54–5
needs theory 30
The New School for Social Research 16
Nietzsche, Fredrick 6, 46
Noddings, Nel 70
norms 15, 36, 53, 88–9, 103, 122

O

Obama, Barack 16
objectives-based education 50, 66–7
operant conditioning 27, 36

P

Palmer, Parker 57, 59, 71–2, 147
paradigm of agency 52
Pavlov, Ivan 27, 32, 54
Pedagogy 51–61, 110, 118, 121, 132
  constructivist 56
  critical 58–9
  hidden 52–3
  humanist 55
  Pedagogy of the oppressed (book) 48
  scientific 54
  vocational 57–8
perturbation theory 27
Pert, Candice 116
Peung, Sophie 96
Piaget, Jean-Paul 40, 56, 125, 134
placebo response 116
planned ignoring 29–31
positive reinforcement 29, 76
post-colonial 59
Post-It note 15, 78
post-traumatic stress disorder (PTSD) 73, 86–8
The Power of mindful learning (book) 73, 94
praise 29, 79, 114, 120
prefrontal cortices 87
Primum non nocere 90

Principles of Curriculum and Instruction (book) 54, 66–7
problem-based approach 40
professional development (PD) 10, 53
pro-queer 59
Psychological Reports 111
Psychological Review 20
The Psychology of being (book) 31
psychomotor domain 19
Pygmalion in the classroom (book) 111

Q

Quaker 57

R

Race to the Top (RTT) 98
reciprocal expectation effect 114
resolute awareness 48–65
Retinoblastoma 109
Rogers, Carl 29, 40, 55
Rosenthal, Robert 107–8, 110–12, 114
Rotter, Julian 28, 113
Rousseau, Jean-Jacque 57
Ruiz, Don Miguel 44–5, 121
Ryan, Richard 35–6, 39

S

sacred dialogic tension 48, 65
School Journal 72
Seifert, Tim 39
SEL (Social and Emotional Learning) 5, 13–23
SEL4US (The Social and Emotional Learning Alliance of the United States) 19
Self-actualization 16, 36
Self-determination 33, 37
self-efficacy theory 44, 55, 116

self-management strategies 14
self-regulation 14, 33, 86, 121, 126
silver bullets 30
social and emotional learning 5, 13–23
social classism 59
social learning theory 27
social skills 14, 126
Socrates 52, 57
Skinner, B.F. 27, 29, 32, 54–5
Slingerland, Edward 133
standardized tests 7–8, 20, 129
Stanford University 108
student well-being 14
subcortical sensory system 100
synchronicity 11, 134

T

Talks to Teachers on Psychology 66, 68, 84
Tao te ching 37
Taoism 37
teachable moment 130–8
teacher-centered 40, 57
teacher expectation 110–14
theory of motivation 21
Thich Nhat Hanh 78
Thorndike, Edward 2, 28–32, 52, 54–5, 69
Tomlinson, Carol Ann 40
transactional 49, 64
transcendence 33, 66
transference 5, 30
transfer goals 55
trauma 3–4, 28, 73, 83–90, 102, 133
triadic reciprocal determinism 55
triggered 5, 88, 90, 100, 102
trust 4, 11, 15, 18, 22, 28–9, 35, 39, 47, 50, 63–5, 70–1, 84, 89, 104–5, 117–19, 121, 127, 139–40, 142
Trying not to Try: The Art and Science of Spontaneity (Book) 38
Tyler, Ralph 54–69
Tyler Rationale 54

U

University of Auckland 96
University of Chicago 18, 29, 38
University of Minnesota 112
University of North Carolina-Chapel Hill 94
"The Use of Force" 32, 41, 65, 83, 103–4

V

Value Added Measures (VAM) 98
van der Kolk, Bessel 87
vocational education 57–8
vocationalism 58
vocational pedagogy 57–8
vulnerability 11, 61, 63, 65, 121, 133
Vygotsky, Lev 38, 40, 52, 56, 125

W

Watson, John 27, 31–2, 54
Wesley, John 26
Wiggins, Grant 55, 66
Williams, Robin 16
Williams, Serena 16
Williams, William Carlos 83–6
Winfrey, Oprah 16
wu wei 37–41, 142

Y

YouTube 79, 122

Z

zero-sum game 3, 129
zone of proximal development (ZPD) 38
Zinn, Howard 59

www.ingramcontent.com/pod-product-compliance
Lightning Source LLC
Chambersburg PA
CBHW061716300426
44115CB00014B/2718